"It is an honor to lh in any capacity. Those that work in church ministry are a unique breed of individuals that often sacrifice personal ambition to serve others with great compassion. Most young ministers that jump into pastoral ministry find themselves working in another career after only a few short years and more than 1,500 leave the ministry every month. Blue Collar Pastor is a reminder to every individual that serves in the church that you are significant to the kingdom of God and you are making an impact in this world."

- *Larry Ellis, Senior Pastor of Abundant Life Church*

Larry's authentic childhood stories will entertain you, inspire you, encourage you, and challenge you to wonder if your life with God could likewise be filled with great moments. This collection of real life episodes with snapshots of life growing up in a country pastor's family: the laughs and the struggles, the setbacks and the breakthroughs. It's an entertaining blend of *Huck Finn* meets *It's a Wonderful Life*. Here's your chance to be a fly on the wall of a pioneering family that built their corner of the Kingdom of God, and loved it.

- *Pastor Tyler Daniels, fellow blue-collar pastor*

This book is dedicated to my family. In my Father's memory, and for the ministry for which he fought so hard; to Mom, who was by his side during the victories and defeats, and from whom I learned faithfulness no matter the cost; to Pam, my beloved wife, who has endured some of the greatest struggles in ministry with me as well as celebrated our greatest achievements, especially our four boys; to my sister Amy, who has diligently worked in ministry with me, and with whom I have so many cherished childhood memories; to my younger brother Dan, whom I loved dearly as a baby and grew to respect as a talented and faithful man; and to my four sons and daughter-in-law. As you go through life's journey, I hope you will always remember where you came from and treasure your own stories.

Contents

4 Introduction

Grand Haven, Michigan (1970-1972)
10 Sand Dunes and Barrels
15 Cats and Sisters
19 Nursery Fires and Praying Dads

Sault Ste. Marie, Michigan (1972-1974)
24 Big Dogs and Garage Church
28 Trailers and Bloody Ears

Sheridan, Michigan (1974-1976)
33 The Lone Ranger and Spinning Brothers
38 Steeples and Preaching to the Choir
42 Flying Squirrels and a Spoonful of Mustard

Ohio Buckeye (1976-1979)
48 Superheroes and Hillbillies
52 Flowers for Mom and Turtles for Boys
56 Popcorn and Girl Power 1
61 Paper Routes and a 1979 Selfie
54 Spinning Cars and Change of Plans

Twin Lake, Michigan (1978-1979)
72 Fried Chicken & Grandma's Eyes
76 Dump Trucks and Blown Transmissions
80 Road Trips and Sisters

Montana 1 (1979-1983)
85 Grizzly Bears and Girl Power 2
90 Guns, Porcupine Cuisine and Fried Rabbit
95 Burning Dads and Sliding Chihuahuas
99 Noisy Kids and Superman
103 Blackfoot Basketball and Humiliation
107 Big Bikes and Sister's Scars
112 Brass Has Class
118 Bon Fires and Peppermint Schnapps

Montana 2
123 Whiskey, Ginger, and Girl Power 3
127 Noodles and Skunks
132 Cow Tipping and a Jail Break
137 Pig Pens and Apple Fights
141 Freshman and Fighting
146 Exploding Gas Cans and Screaming Moms
150 Pump Organs and Ceiling Fans

Enumclaw, Washington (1983-1989)
154 Big City Blues
159 Jesus Freaks and Evolution
163 Camps and Calling
167 High School Pain and Girl Power 4
172 Falling Out of Trees and Into Love
177 Swing Sets and Hammers

Misery or Missouri? (1989-1991)
186 Busted Pipes and Flooded Bookstores
182 From Misery to Ministry

The Oregon Trail (1991-1994)
194 Drano Bombs and Maturity
200 Chasing Sheep and Baby Boys
205 From Interim to Pastor

Lakewood, Washington (1995-Present)
209 Scuba and Diapers
213 Preaching to Cats
217 Rumor Weeds and Biting Sheep
223 Boards and Dads
227 Dads and Devic's
232 Heart Attacks and Priorities

237 For What It's Worth
(Wisdom for life and ministry)

Introduction

Pastors and their families serving in churches, are underappreciated. Popular culture typically envisions stadiums filled with people emptying their wallets for a slick-speaking preacher selling salvation along with their latest book. Yet reality is much different. The average congregation in America's churches is about eighty people. Of all churches in America, mega-churches make up less than one-half of one percent. What is amazing to me is the pastors of these small churches are more like paid volunteers than staff members. The average salary for ministers of small congregations hovers near the poverty level.

Being a pastor of any church has its challenges, but leading a small congregation of under two-hundred people can be a demanding job as well as a rewarding one. I grew up in a home with two of the most amazing people who chose to pursue this calling, my Mom and Dad. This book is a compilation of short stories from my life growing up in a family strong enough to answer the call to love the church, and brave enough to be pastors.

Small rural churches can have great influence in their communities and have the potential to produce the most meaningful relationships on the planet. People can feel connected with a greater sense of unity in a small church. They can find places to serve, and thrive as followers of Jesus because of the love and acceptance the church offers. Today, larger churches are asking how they can "do church smaller" because of the increasing need to connect with people on a personal level. Just because a church is small doesn't mean that the quality of ministry is poor or that there will be nothing to learn from it. At least it doesn't have to be that way.

I have been the Senior Pastor of Abundant Life Church in Lakewood, Washington since 1995. The church, like many churches its size, is an amazing group of people. They serve one another and grow in relationship with Christ, while enjoying rich relationships with one another and loving the church as a whole. We eat together, play together and pray together. The church regularly sends out teams to minister throughout many foreign countries. We support missionaries and serve our community, give to the needy, and do what we can to impact our world. The church has regular outreach events to serve our community. We have a web presence that draws thousands of people to our sermons. We produce music, develop curriculum, and write books, all from a church that is far from "big." Our size is insignificant to our mission; to love God an others well, thrive in life, connect with people, and to serve others. We hold a simple belief that we are stewards simply using all that God has entrusted to us.

This book is written to inspire and encourage all those who plant churches or lead and minister in small established congregations. You are astounding! You are the unsung hero of the pastoral world. While Christendom may applaud the large ministries, remain focused on the basic purposes of the ministry - to love people and make disciples. Church growth fads will come and go, don't wear yourself out by trying to keep up! Larger churches may plant churches all around you, they might create multi-sites, or fully-support multiple programs, and that is ok! We should be thankful for their work; I know I am. Small church pastors should never apologize for their church having fewer members than any other church. We are simply called to make disciples; God will do the rest. We must fuel a desire for growth that is more than numbers, or transfers from one church to another.

"I'd rather spend half an hour in the company of a top carpenter, than three hours in the company of an average brain surgeon."
Winston Churchill

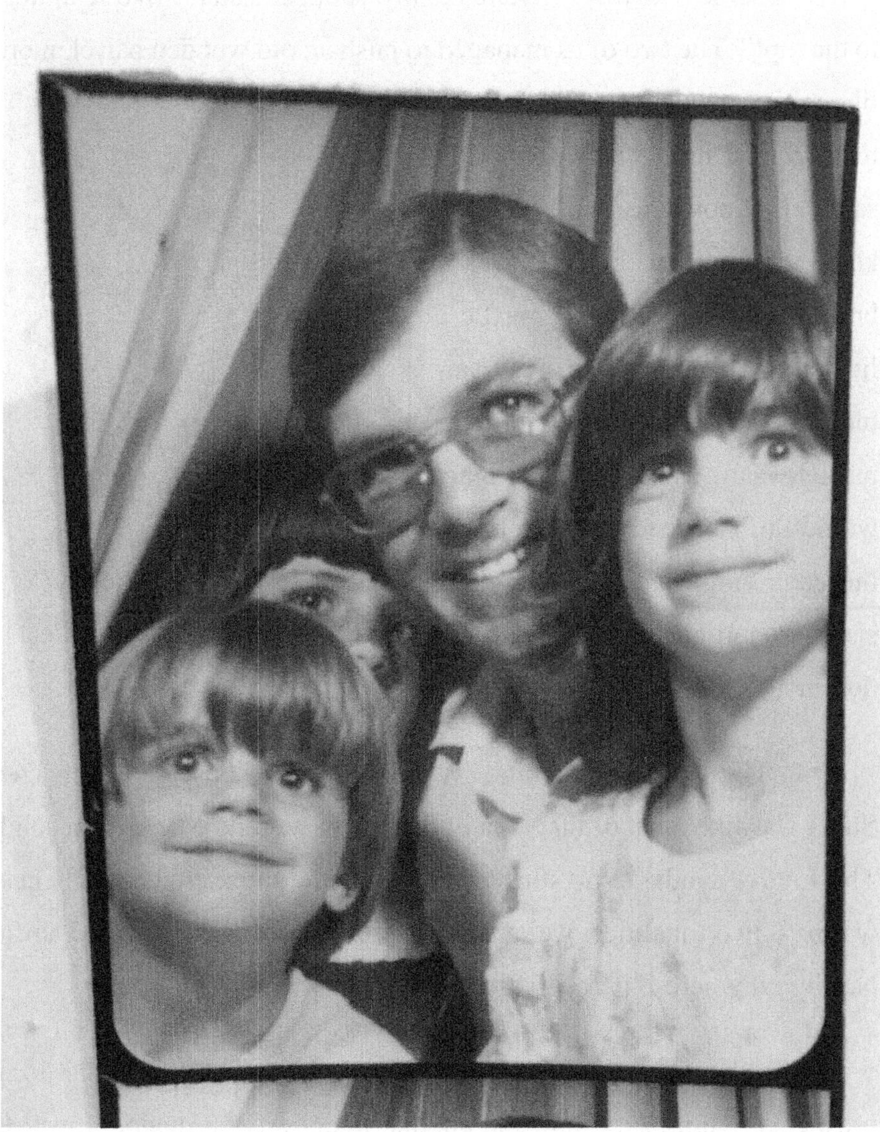

Sand Dunes and Barrels

"Come on, Amy!" I yelled to my younger sister. "We're almost to the top!" The two of us managed to push an old wooden barrel, more like a big bucket, all the way up to the top of a hill. "Now get in," I said. I'm not sure Amy was too keen on the idea, but she was a brave three-year-old, and maybe a little too trusting of her five-year-old brother. She crawled into the bucket, and as any big brother would do, I pushed the barrel over the edge and watched it fling my sister around and around like a rag doll in a clothes dryer.

The sand dunes behind my grandparents' house on Beach Tree Street was like most of that area of Michigan with its pale golden sand. This kind of sand doesn't stick to you and in the summer, it actually gets warm - two qualities we are hard-pressed to find in the Pacific Northwest where I live with my family.

With eyes wide I watched as Amy rolled down the hill, her long brown hair flung sand into the air like a sideways tornado. Ensuing screams sent me running after her to see what kind of injuries I had caused. Yes, we did dangerous things like this without a helmet and we are still alive. Fortunately for me, when she finally came to a stop, she was ok. Believe it or not she was perfectly fine, other than her clothes, her shoes, her hair, her face and the rest of her being covered with sand. There wasn't a scratch on her, although she looked dazed, like she had been through the spin cycle in a clothes washer. Once we got back to the house, I received what would become the usual consequences of my actions from Dad; a careful explanation of why I was being punished, then the commencing of the corporal punishment.

Mom and Dad's strong faith in Christ was substantial and obvious. Like Amy being tossed around that barrel, sometimes it felt like as a family we were flung far and wide to plant churches. As a family we were immersed in the church ministry in many ways; our upbringing as kids revolved around the church and its ministry every day. It was not uncommon see my dad with a hammer in one hand and Bible in the other, figuratively speaking. Dad was always bi-vocational, working as a pastor while maintaining a full-time job to support the church and his ministry. Mom was equally as hard-working and held a variety of different jobs, from working at the bank to cleaning houses, in addition to serving in some capacity in the church. The churches they led varied from small churches that started in our living room to established congregations.

As the saying goes, we were born on Saturday and in church on Sunday, and we were never late. If the doors were open, we were there. I know it had to be very challenging at times for my parents; church ministry takes a lot of effort working with people and their issues, managing the finances and maintaining buildings. But through all the hard work Dad's faith was always visible. It wasn't uncommon to hear my dad worship while playing the piano, praying out loud or working on one of the various projects that always seemed to need doing. As a young teenager I began to be resentful because of all the work, money, and the time and energy we poured into the church. I would often wonder why we always had to go to churches that were small and couldn't support Mom and Dad, or why we had to start something from scratch with no help. I would eventually find myself at odds with ministry in general because I compared it to other careers. It wasn't until years later when I heard the same call as my parents that I finally understood what all the hard work and sacrifice was about.

FOR WHAT IT'S WORTH

The genuine call of God will always be bigger and require more than your abilities.

- Move forward boldly with God's call, it didn't come from you. God is the One who has called you, not you.
- Don't worry about the work being beyond your talent because God will equip you for the task.
- You will question your calling, however, never offer questions without listening for answers.
- Don't allow your failures to dampen moving ahead. You can't move forward if you keep looking back, you can't think about the future when haunted by the past.

"For God's gifts and His call are irrevocable"... Romans 11:29

Cats and Sisters

The usual punishment growing up was commonly a good old-fashioned spanking and being sent upstairs to think about what we had done and to take a nap. To a small child, this was cruel and unusual punishment; but we managed to make the best of it. What was intended to be repentance and reflection on our transgressions became a covert playtime. Amy and I started our sentence out quietly but soon advanced to horseplay. Eventually, we were jumping on the bed, the noise of the bedsprings squeaking, threatening to give us away.

"Somebody's coming!" one of us would loudly whisper when we thought we heard footsteps coming up the stairs. Quick as we could, we would fling ourselves down and throw a blanket over us; stifling giggles while pretending to be asleep. We were laughing out loud a minute later when we realized there was no one there.

One afternoon we were on the bed when all of the sudden we heard,

"Meow."

"What's that?" Amy asked.

"It's a cat somewhere."

We both jumped off of the bed and went to the open window. Next to the house, there was a large oak tree. The tree was close enough to the house that it barely brushed the windowsill. Looking and searching intently through the branches I saw it. "It's a cat," I said to my sister. From the boughs of the tree, a tabby looked straight at us. He stared back at us, and then promptly ignored us, as any good cat would. I stood there watching the cat prowling behind the leaves and stalking from limb to limb; Amy ran over to the nightstand and grabbed what was left of the peanut butter and jelly sandwich she brought up with her.

"Here," she said, handing me her sandwich. I took it and held it out for the cat. After about a thousand "Here, kitty-kitties," we were able to entice our soon to be hostage to the window and grab him. We quickly closed the window cutting off his chance of any escape. Fortunately for us, he was a friendly cat and didn't seem to mind our company, and after all he was eating a good sandwich.

"Hey, Amy, did you know that cats always land on their feet?" "Open the window," I said. Amy ran to the window to open it. "I'm going to throw the cat out the window and we'll see if it lands on its feet." The impending incident would have given any animal rights activist a massive coronary event. I picked up the cat and held it out of the window as we started our countdown,

"Ten,"

"nine,"

"eight,"

"seven,"

"six,"

"five,"

"four… " "WHAT are you kids doing?"

Amy and I were so focused on the scientific breakthroughs we were about to make that the booming voice of our uncle Roy almost scared us out of our skins. Uncle Roy's intervention saved the cat. We, however, were not so fortunate. After freeing the cat from its captivity, Uncle Roy turned us in to the authorities (Mom and Dad) and we were punished. Amy, less an assistant and more the curious on-looker, escaped fairly unscathed. I on the other hand wasn't so fortunate, receiving the full extent of Dad's discipline. (Looking back now, we deserved the punishment we received.)

FOR WHAT IT'S WORTH

God's call to the ministry births vision and may often interrupt your plans.

- Don't be surprised if God changes your plans.
- Don't resent the authorities that God puts in your life that seem to challenge the plan. They are only the tools that God will use to direct you.
- Be accountable by being correctable.
- Hear everyone, but only listen to those humble enough to walk with you.

"The plans of the righteous are just, but the advice of the wicked is deceitful."
Proverbs 12:5

Nursery Fires and Praying Dads

It gets cold and snowy in Michigan during the winter and this day was no exception. The entrance to the church in Grand Haven was preceded by cement steps that always seemed to be covered in snow. Dad would take me out to "help" shovel snow off of the steps. After we finished clearing the steps, we would go inside so Dad could attend to what needed doing and to warm up. It was cold inside the church so Dad turned on a little electric heater in the nursery and told me to play while he went into the sanctuary. Having been born into a family of carpenters I looked around and saw all the available material scattered before me. I decided a fort-building adventure was in order. After all, that's one of the things that little boys do when left to their own devices in a nursery. There was a window between the nursery and the sanctuary, so I could occasionally pull the curtain aside and make sure where Dad was and what he was doing.

I got busy building my masterpiece. I got a blanket and tied one corner to the handle of the heater, another end got tied to a corner of the baby crib. I set a pile of song books down to hold the third corner of the blanket and propped up the middle with a broom handle while the fourth corner hung down to make a flap for the entrance. I completed my fort and it was glorious. But something happened in that moment that happens to many young boys who get wrapped up in what they are doing and don't pay attention to nature's call. I had to pee, and bad. I didn't want to leave my new fortress of solitude, I had to put it off. I danced around as long as I could until I dashed out of the nursery where I found relief in the bathroom across the hall. When I got back to the nursery, the broom handle had fallen down and the heater was under the blanket, which was on fire! I ran out of the nursery, straight up to the piano, grabbed Dad's arm, "Daddy, Daddy!" I might as well have been the sole Cleveland Browns' fan at Gillette Stadium watching the Patriots win the Super Bowl, again. Dad was in a stadium of his own, lost in the Spirit. My attempts to get his attention, needless to say, did very little. I ran back to the nursery to check on my little conflagration, and then back to the sanctuary to try to get Dad's attention. Back to the nursery and then to the sanctuary. To the nursery. To the sanctuary. Finally, I just yelled out, "Daddy look!" My dad stopped and opened his eyes. That was when he saw the very visible flames through the nursery window. I've never seen my dad run so fast, before or since. He took care of the fire in short order, grabbing a blanket and smothering the fire until the flames subsided. Expecting the spanking I thought I would get, Dad took me aside. But I didn't get a spanking, however I did get a thorough and sincere in-depth amount of instruction that fire doesn't care what it burns, and how dangerous that can be.

I will always remember my dad's sincerity not only in his instruction but also in his prayers and worship. He did it so fervently, often raising his hands when he prayed, or closing his eyes and singing loudly at the piano. He would have such a genuine spiritual experience; it was truly beautiful to watch. In my teenage years Dad would get up very early in the morning. Before he left for work, and sitting in his chair, he would read his Bible and pray. He would also pray with me at night. If it was late, he would often come in and put his hand on me and pray. I know he did this because there were times when I would pretend to be sleeping and feel him rest his hand on me and hear his whispered prayer. He would then turn around and do the same for my little brother.

FOR WHAT IT'S WORTH

Your first ministry is not to people, church budgets, broken toilets, or building funds, it is to Christ.

- It is impossible to truly minister to others without ministering to God. You were called to serve Him first. Pray and worship Him daily.
- You can deliver sermons without prayer, but you cannot preach without prayer.
- No Christian should be a worship leader, rather they should be the lead worshipper.
- It is disingenuous to tell others of the goodness of God when you have not experienced it yourself.
- God is the One building the church. The people are following Him, not you.

"God is Spirit, and those who worship Him must worship in spirit and truth."
John 4:24

"If you can't fly, then run, if you can't run, then walk, if you can't walk, then crawl, but whatever you do, you have to keep moving forward."
Martin Luther King Jr.

Big Dogs and Garage Church

"Look, it's not that far," my mom said, pointing down the street to the school, two blocks away. I had been accustomed to walking to school with her hand-in-hand, but now for the first time I had to walk alone. With my little sister at home Mom wouldn't have to pack both of us two blocks down the street to kindergarten. The issue for me wasn't that is was very far for a six-year-old, but that there was a great beast along the way, one of enormous size that intimidated me greatly, big teeth, a ferocious growl and glaring eyes. It was by far the meanest creature alive, The Beast – A Beagle! I was so intimidated by The Beast that I pleaded with Mom to walk with me, so of course she did, but that only took care of the way to school; I knew I still had to walk home alone. I spent the whole day dreading the fact that this was going to happen whether I liked it or not.

When school was finally out, I knew my time had come and I would have to face The Beast. I put on my coat, grasped my metal lunchbox firmly in hand and headed down the sidewalk facing the two agonizing blocks to get home. In the distance I could hear Mom calling me and see her waving at me. That was good, at least I had the destination in view. Each step took me closer and closer to my house; but also brought me closer to The Beast. I didn't want to look up, so I kept my head down. "Keep looking down, keep looking down," I kept reciting to myself. All at once I looked up and back, and my greatest fears were realized. The Beast was on the loose and was running after me! My heart pounded as I sprinted toward Mom's voice, hoping to outrun the dog nipping at my heels. Then it happened, with a terrific jump The Beast landed on me and knocked me down. I was terrified! My eyes were closed; I was too afraid to move. All I could think about was whether or not I was going to get eaten. And if I did what would it feel like? I just lay there crying and terrified as The Beast relentlessly licked my face. The next thing I know strong arms are lifting me up. Mom was holding me securely in her arms, her voice soothing and consoling as we made our way home. I will never forget that day, Mom was my hero who had come and saved me from The Beast.

She wasn't the only hero in our home, she shared that title with another. Our house in Sault Ste. Marie, Michigan, was on a fairly busy street with a good sized yard where I would play. My dad built the church he was planting in Sault Ste. Marie, right beside our house. It was a simple structure, just like a garage. It was probably about twenty-four by forty feet. It had a side entry with bathrooms and the little sanctuary that had an oil burning stove in the back of the room. Dad's brothers didn't always agree with his ministry direction, but they did come up and help Dad build the church. They totally enclosed the building in one day's work.

Planting a church in those days was tough, it still is! In the early days there weren't any supporting churches or any other kind of help. The work was left to the planter, their family and all the volunteers he could muster. Dad built new buildings just about everywhere we went. Starting a church from scratch needs a place to meet, and as the church planters it was up to Mom and Dad to arrange for that meeting place, which meant that they did everything from constructing the building to pastoring, to leading in a variety of capacities. Dad would play piano, and he and Mom would sing. Mom's songs are some of the most memorable things I can recall from those days. She has such a rich alto voice, and I was convinced she knew every song ever written. They trusted God and worked hard. Mom and Dad were pioneers, the progenitors of the church we have today. They literally laid the foundations of the church building as well as the congregation.

FOR WHAT IT'S WORTH

Planting churches is God's idea.

- When you are the only one that shows up for a work day, work.
- You may not have the talent to do some things, do them anyway. Anything done is better than nothing.
- If it has to be done, you do it. As others join in the mission, let them do it. Rejoice when they succeed and give grace when they fail.
- Your work planting a small church is no less significant or of lower importance than any large church.
- Never expect or wait for the support of others. God has called you, they haven't. He will build His church.

"According to the grace of God given to me, like a skilled master builder I laid a foundation, and someone else is building upon it. Let each one take care how he builds upon it."
1 Corinthians 3:10

Trailers and Bloody Ears

Mom called out, "Larry Jack, it's time for your haircut." Dad always cut my hair growing up, it was kind of a guy thing to do. I hopped up on the chair with about ten songbooks piled up so I could sit up higher and be easier for my Dad to reach. "Now be still," he would say. Well, I apparently wasn't still enough because the scissors not only cut my hair but sliced right through part of my earlobe. I think Dad was surprised at first because I had no reaction until I saw the blood on the towel he was using to stop the bleeding. Blood! My blood! Then came the tears. Mom came over and put a bandage on my ear which was quite large. Ok, it was very large. I remember going into the bathroom and looking in the mirror at this huge bandage. It certainly made it look much worse than it really was. But then, maybe large bandages were all we had to work with.

Shortly after being wounded, Amy and I went out to play in the front yard, in an old, little single-axle trailer that we had. The trailer was short, and had plywood sides that we could barely see over. It was the perfect size for us to have a fun place to hide and goof around.

"What happened to your ear?" an older boy asked me as he walked by our house.

"My dad cut it off."

"What? The whole thing?" He said.

"No. He was cutting my hair and cut my ear so I have this bandage on it."

"Amy!" my mom's voice came from the back door, "Time to come in."

"Do you want to play?" I asked the older boy as my sister started toward the house.

"Sure." He said.

We started running around hopping in and out of the trailer. He was older than me and outweighed me by at least 20 pounds. When he hopped on the back of the trailer it flipped over, there was a loud noise and a big cloud of dust followed by darkness. I was in the wrong place at the wrong time and now I was trapped under the trailer.

"Lift it up!" I yelled.

No answer.

"Lift it up!" I yelled again.

Nothing.

He had taken off and left me there. Not only had he left me there, but after that day, I never saw him again.

I was terrified, but I was determined to get out. I banged on the sides of the trailer, I yelled and tried to lift it, but it was too heavy. At that point my mind took over and as any young boy does, I started thinking, "what if I have to go the bathroom in here? That would be gross. What if Mom makes dinner and I'm not there to eat. Will I starve?" My imagination was going strong and for what seemed like hours, but was actually only minutes, at last I heard Dad's voice.

"Larry Jack! Where are you?"

"Daddy!" I said, "I'm under the trailer!"

It was a relief that I didn't have to use the bathroom under there, which would have been bad, and I never did find out what happens when you starve. One thing I will never forget is the darkness disappearing as blinding daylight flooded in when Dad lifted up that trailer and pulled me out. I could always trust Dad to be there and save the day, with helping hand or lesson well taught.

FOR WHAT IT'S WORTH

Trust God no matter what!

- Just because you may question your situation never means that God is not with you.
- Feeling alone NEVER means that you are. The Christ-follower is always in the company of the Savior.
- Fear is a genuine indicator that we have traded trusting God for being overwhelmed by our circumstances.
- Feelings of being trapped, alone and forgotten will come. Toughen up, pull up your bootstraps, this won't last, trust God. The darkness will be overcome with the light.

"He will never leave you nor forsake you.
Do not be afraid; do not be discouraged."
Deuteronomy 31:8

John Adams was a farmer, Abraham Lincoln a small town lawyer. Plato and Socrates were teachers. Jesus was a carpenter. To equate wisdom with occupation is at best insulting.

The Lone Ranger and Spinning Brothers

"Mom! Is it on yet?" I must have asked my mom that same question over and over at least a hundred times every afternoon. I just couldn't wait and then, finally, it was on - the highlight of the day - The Lone Ranger. This was NOT the television version, but the RADIO one. Yep, a big brown box with knobs and dials and tan cloth over speakers on each side. The one where your imagination acts out the adventure in full color in your mind.

There wasn't much to do in Sheridan, Michigan in the winter, except stay inside to keep warm and try to entertain yourself to keep the boredom away. We must have made Mom crazy when the school bus didn't run and school was cancelled because of snow, which in those days didn't actually happen as much as a school age boy could want. But, when we got snow, boy did we get snow! Several feet in fact, every winter. To this day I love getting snowed-in, especially if the power goes out. I know it's crazy, there's just something about building a fire, using candles and playing board games that's cozy to me. The two redeeming factors for me in those days were my train set, which I could play with for hours, and The Lone Ranger radio program. And was it a show! There were sound effects of horses running, guns shooting, spurs... uh... spurring. I would listen intently as Amy ran around with the newest one-year-old addition to the tribe, our brother, Danny. All too soon the program would be over and I was off to find a new adventure to keep me occupied.

When the Lone Ranger show was over Amy and I decided to take our little brother to the den. This room was enclosed with windows everywhere and looked out onto a wrap-around porch. It was also the room where we had the piano with a spinning piano stool. We parked Danny on that stool and Amy and I looked out at all that snow. Granted, in Michigan snow was nothing new, but fresh snow, now that's a whole different story. Fresh snow brought a whole new landscape that we would look at for what seemed like hours. Danny didn't look out of the windows being only a year old, but he sure enjoyed sitting on the piano stool. Amy and I were learning that the usual activity for our one-year-old little brother was to keep his older brother and sister from having any fun by going everywhere he wasn't allowed to be and getting into everything he wasn't allowed to have. Fortunately, we had learned that Danny was happy to sit on that piano stool and stay there. We soon realized he liked the piano stool because it spun around. So, being the good brother and sister that we were, we started to spin him, and spin him, and spin him, around and around and around, until we were the very shocked and miserable recipients of his explosive regurgitation. Mom would come and scold us for making him sick and then begin the task of cleaning up the mess we had caused. We were definitely a lot of work for mom.

I believe those days weren't easy, especially for Mom and Dad – long days filled with work, ministry and raising three kids and the financial hardships that come along with planting a church and keeping the family afloat. Dad was a skilled carpenter, but carpentry is an occupation that usually occurs outside. Doing work outside in central Michigan was nearly impossible during a couple of months every year for most people. However, my dad would work during the winter months when the average temperature was 20 degrees. I will never forget one winter day saying goodbye to him as he walked through the long snow-filled driveway to head south to work with one of his brothers on a house somewhere. Things were tight, Dad would go wherever he could to work. There was a time that we only had canned tomatoes and fried bread to eat. We called it "Indian Bread," with a little butter on it, it was heaven on earth.

Leading a small church can be a huge financial burden, that hasn't changed. Today, someone can make more as a Walmart greeter than they could pastoring a small church. Without dedicated people answering the call at all cost, sacrificing their time, their money, and the prospect for an easier life, the church in America would not exist. I believe the greatest people on earth are found in these ministers and their families and deserve to be celebrated much more in Christendom.

FOR WHAT IT'S WORTH
Church ministry can bring big financial pressures.

- Embrace bi-vocational ministry. To take care of the needs of your family you're probably going to need to get a job.
- Just because you work a second job does not mean your ministry is not fruitful or a "success" as defined by your denominational leadership.
- If you are a bi-vocational minister in a small church or plant, you are a hero! The determination and strength in you to do what needs to be done comes from God and obeying the call. See it through, no matter the cost!
- I would personally love to hear you preach more than the most "successful" pastor in the world.

> "A good man brings good things out of the good stored up in him, and an evil man brings evil things out of the evil stored up in him."
> Matthew 12:35

Steeples and Preaching to the Choir

"Hold on tight," Dad said as he let go of the rope. There is nothing more fun than holding on for your life as you become the overmatched counterweight to a large steeple bell. It's the closest I could get to the power of flight. Up, up and away I went in that steeple. It may have looked like an ordinary traditional steeple but I knew the truth, there is nothing traditional about the flight I could take in its walls. The bigger the steeple the better the flight.

The church in Sheridan was an old, traditional-looking church building with a big steeple and wooden pews. We lived just up the hill from the church so getting back and forth was normally easy. One winter we got much more snow than usual, so much that nobody, not one single person, came to church one Sunday. Well, no one that is, except for Amy, Danny, myself and of course, Mom and Dad. We were all there, groomed, dressed up and ready for service. As we sat in the pew waiting to see if anyone would show up, it didn't take long for us to realize that even the snow-hardened Michiganders weren't going to make it through the drifts of snow that had piled up. Dad stood up and walked up to the pulpit and began the service. He started by leading us in singing *'Victory in Jesus'* and just as though it was a full congregation sitting there, he then preached, to the four of us.

I couldn't tell you what the message was about, what text he used, or how well he delivered the sermon. All I know is that he followed through, he did his work. No matter how few or many there were he held true to his calling and pastored any who came. Mom and Dad's first disciples were Amy and Danny, and myself. This is the day it started for me. Their dedication and ministry that day produced a follower of Christ who would one day also be a pastor who would be able to endure the hardships of ministry.

I believe that just as my parents' faith influenced me, my grandparents' faith influenced Dad. My grandpa Ellis had a crazy-love for Jesus. He was the real deal, just as my dad was and I try to be. I think by today's standards he would be considered completely radical. He sure was back then. You could often see him out in the driveway where he would stop suddenly to worship with his hands lifted and speaking in tongues. He would also begin praying out loud, no matter where he was or who was around, and would tell everyone about Jesus and I mean everyone, no matter their age, occupation, gender, or economic status. Everyone! I really wish I could have spoken to him more when I was a bit older. There are so many things I could have learned from him. I would have especially liked to have asked him questions about his noticeably intimate relationship with Jesus. I believe he understood eternity with clarity and lived his life to that end. He had no theological training, no refined apologetic arguments, or a Bible degree. He simply had Jesus. It was his zeal for the Lord that I remember most. My dad had a similar zeal and fire for the Lord - one I too try to live visibly.

FOR WHAT IT'S WORTH

Preach the Word

- Trust the Bible to take care of itself. Simply read it, boldly proclaim it, and trust it to do the work.
- Tell the Gospel simply, teach the Bible plainly, and preach the Word faithfully.
- Others may stretch it, reorganize it, repackage it and sell it, you simply teach it.
- Preach the Word, especially when it may seem inconvenient, no matter the size of the congregation or the social makeup of your audience.

"Preach the word; be ready in season and out of season; reprove, rebuke, and exhort, with complete patience and teaching."
2 Timothy 4:2

Flying Squirrels and a Spoonful of Mustard

"It's a nice size piece of property," my dad said to the potential buyers of our house. Once again, we were getting ready to move - this time to give Dad more work opportunities. My dad gave the people a guided tour of the property, pointing out all the positive aspects of the house. They inspected the garage and walked around the yard, looking at the large oak trees that were in the center of our circle driveway. I really liked those trees; I had spent many hours outside playing in the leaves and throwing rocks at the flying squirrels that dominated them. Somehow, maybe to escape dangerous projectiles flung at them by a mischievous seven-year-old, they took up residence in the attic of the house. My sister and I could hear them at night, it sounded like the squirrels were rolling acorns from one side of the attic to the other.

Dad, and the people he was talking with had almost finished a tour of the yard and were talking about some of the features of the property when I suddenly shocked him by speaking up and saying, "And there are flying squirrels living in the attic." The look on my dad's face went from pleasant and friendly to dark and foreboding. I had seen that look on my dad's face before and quickly ran into the house, making my escape. I was pretty sure I knew what was coming next.

Under those big oak trees in the middle of the circular driveway was where we parked our car. It was a massive, four-door, green, Gran Torino. In those days a car seat for toddlers and children was your mother's lap and seat belts were straps that you pushed down into the seats of the car. And watch out, in the summer you risked being branded by the metal parts of the buckle if they were sitting in direct sunlight and you happened to sit on them or pick them up. One day, Mom was taking Amy with her to the store. She started the car and then put Amy in the passenger seat. Having remembered something, Mom went back into the house for a minute, but a minute can be a long time and Amy got bored and decided that the running car was a good place to explore. When Mom came back the car was missing, it wasn't in the driveway! Being the intrepid explorer Amy had managed to put the car in gear and drive it right into the ditch, and all without a license - which I found quite awesome. Yep, those trees have some incredible memories for me, and I'm really glad they and the squirrels couldn't talk.

One day, in that same house, Dad and I were alone. I was playing with my toys and Dad was somewhere else in the house. I was off in my own little world of cars and trucks when I was brought back to reality by the smell of cooking meat. I followed the aroma to the kitchen where Dad was frying bologna for sandwiches. The aroma, steam and the sizzle from the pan were familiar in our house. We were far from well off, but my mom and dad were able to take humble ingredients and make them into the most delightful cuisine. One of those being fried baloney sandwiches which were a common lunch for us.

Dad had all of the ingredients on the counter in front of him. The bread was still in its wrapper so that it would be as fresh as possible. There was bologna in the pan and some more on a plate, ready for the frying pan. Next to the butter there was a jar I didn't recognize. It looked a little like ketchup, but it was yellow. I like ketchup. What kid doesn't? I went to the silverware drawer and got a spoon. My dad was watching me out of the corner of his eye, and wasn't surprised when I asked, "Dad, can I eat this?" The look in my dad's eye and the smirk on his face should have warned me as he said "Why, yes."

I put the spoonful of mustard in my mouth, and at once knew why my dad was trying not to smile. As my body was trying to decide the quickest way of eliminating this evil substance from my mouth and my mind was reminding me not to spit out food, my dad was trying not to laugh. I grabbed the closest glass I could and began drinking glass after glass of water; my dad was trying not to cry because he was laughing so hard. It is interesting how something so yellow turned me so green. I know that it was nothing other than a prank, but I really believe to this day that my dad was getting a bit of payback for my comment about squirrels in the attic.

Leaving Sheridan, Michigan as kid was not a major event, and leaving the church there was no big deal. As an adult, I have often thought about how it all must have affected Mom and Dad. Whether or not for them it may have been "good riddance," or if maybe they were sad to go; I don't believe that we've ever talked about it. I do know, however, that it is God who opens new doors and that my parents were faithful enough to follow and walk through the doors he opened. They trusted God without knowing what was down the next road. For me, Sheridan will always be the place that connected flying squirrels to a spoonful of mustard.

FOR WHAT IT'S WORTH

When you lead a church, your whole family is involved.

- Know when to say "when." Your choices will lead your children to either love the ministry or resent it.
- Your ministry to others begins with your family no matter what your board or church members may believe.
- Pray and praise together, both in the victories and losses in ministry, as a family.
- Shield your family from words or actions that come from both inside and outside the ministry.
- Leaving your children an inheritance of a godly character is worth more than money.

"A cheerful heart is good medicine, but a crushed spirit dries up the bones."
Proverbs 17:22

"It would be far more beneficial for the character of our young men if they were to spend more time on a framing crew versus the university campus."

Superheroes and Hillbillies

"Wait till the smoke clears, then we'll jump out!" Amy and I were in the bathroom pretending to be superheroes. We imagined the room being filled with smoke as we put on our capes, then we'd run out of the bathroom, striking terror into the hearts of imaginary villains as we brought them to justice. Amy and I were the best superheroes we could be and always got our villain. It was one of the few places we could play and we took full advantage of it. It was more difficult to find places to play in our new home in Richmond Dale, Ohio than it was in Michigan. We lived in a mobile home behind the house of our landlord, literally out in the sticks. You may think living in the sticks meant that there would be many uncharted lands we could map out but Mom and Dad didn't want us going off too far and getting lost or hurt. So, much of that great outdoors land had to be left unexplored by a young Amy and myself.

Dad worked as a serviceman for a mobile home company when we lived in Richmond Dale. From time to time I would get to go with him to the various job sites, holding tools, carrying supplies, fetching items I could handle; all good experience for a nine-year-old. We didn't need a "take-your-kid-to-work-day," we were voluntold that's what we were doing. It was just a part of life to be expected to help and learn how to do the things that needed done. Dad was great like a superhero wielding his weapons and making life a little safer for everyone. I was his sidekick on those days, learning the tricks of the trade just like a superhero in training. Ok. Yes, I was only nine. Yes, I used drills and hammers, all without a helmet, safety glasses, or hearing protection and I survived!

Dad was not the pastor of any church while we were at Richmond Dale, but we did attend one, every Sunday, and I loved it. They had puppets! The church there seemed to be full of life and I was enamored with the kids' program. Nothing beats puppets!! There was this one line that our family would repeat and we still use to this day, from time to time. You see, one of the main characters was an alligator who was told by his mom, "How many times have I told you, not to eat the baby ducks." It seemed like the funniest thing to us, and still makes us all crack a smile. While I'm unsure of the context or the spiritual application of this saying, it has stuck with us. All I can say is, we remember what we remember.

The image I have of our landlord and his family was that they were genuine hillbillies. The dad's name was Floyd, and he seemed to spend most of his time on the front porch in a rocking chair. Ordinarily he would be playing a banjo and had a little brown jug by the side of the rocking chair. They had several children and the whole family would gather together and sing folk songs on the porch. I had never seen anything like it, it was fascinating. It wasn't quite a scene from the movie *Deliverance,* but it was close. Imagine a shirtless man with suspender overalls leading a choir of family members with deep Hank Williams roots in the most genuine twang that could possibly exist. Even though they were not church-going people, they still had a certain contentment with life that was unique, at least to me.

Pastoral ministry was on hold for Dad in those days, I think it must have been especially difficult for him. Even though he had responded to God's call, it was evident that is wasn't always clear and easy and often didn't work out the way we all thought it would. I mean, why were we in the backwoods of Ohio seemingly in the middle of nowhere? And why did Dad go to these little tiny churches in the most rural areas of the country? Some of the people were quite difficult. I remember one church where there was a lady that practically ran the place. If Dad preached too long, she would sit in the back, raise her arm up and tap her watch. Some small churches can have their troublemakers, which takes a toll on pastors and too often limits their time there, taking away the ability to make real change. But Dad also believed that the church is God's plan to reach the world. There is no "Plan B." It was a saying long before church growth books hit the market.

FOR WHAT IT'S WORTH

There will be some difficult people in small churches, expect it.

- Immediately confront destructive words and attitudes personally with humility and grace. An offense left open is a festering wound.
- When personal confrontation doesn't work, build a coalition and confront them together.
- When a coalition doesn't work, firmly ask them to leave and stick to your decision. Those that refuse to concede their wrong words and attitudes often will not change.
- The health of a church is more important than its size.

"You were running well. Who hindered you from obeying the truth? This persuasion is not from him who calls you. A little leaven leavens the whole lump."

Galatians 5:7-9

Flowers for Mom and Turtles for Boys

The church in Chillicothe, Ohio was one of my favorite places that Mom and Dad ever served in. One Sunday after church we had lunch at one of our parishioner's homes. I liked it because they had two boys my age to goof around with. "Oh, they'll be alright, they're just going down to the river," the boys' mom said. My mom seemed reluctant to let me go with them, but they expected me to go, and obviously had done this a hundred times before and their mom wasn't concerned with them taking off to the river.

"We have to show you the turtle!"

"What turtle?" I asked them.

"We'll show you."

We ran out of the house toward a very fast-moving river. Once we got to the river, we walked along the banks for quite some time. Eventually we got to the turtle. It was dead! This was my first experience with a large dead animal. And, this one was huge! It looked to be longer than I was tall. It must have been dead for a while because the stink of it was so bad that I almost threw up, but I didn't want to seem like a sissy in front of the other two boys. I just kept looking at the dead turtle, I couldn't help it, and something just pulled at me to keep looking. I remember on the way home thinking about what I had seen, it really impacted me. It was the first time I really thought about death and what it meant. I mean that turtle's life was over, no more tomorrows. That's a pretty heavy thought for a kid. I remember it well because it was the first time I had really thought about life being so finite and short. At nine years old the Sunday school lessons started to mesh with my new reality. I was going to die one day and Jesus is the only one that can save me.

The church in Chillicothe, Ohio was a nice brick building and seemed to be bustling with activity. There was always something going on. Sunday school, prayer meetings, and fellowship of all kinds. I had an awesome Sunday school class and I really liked my teacher. She told the Bible stories with such enthusiasm and sincerity and always wanted to know what was going on with me. The two brothers were also in my class. It was one of the few times growing up that I was in an actual class in church that wasn't taught or led by Mom or Dad. It was spring and we were doing a craft project for Mother's Day. We were given large plastic mugs. They were hollow with foam inside. We put in flowers and colored sticks with words on them for our mothers for Mother's Day. I was thinking how much I hoped that Mom would like it. The teacher asked us who we were giving the mugs to, and one by one around the room each student said their mom, everyone except the two brothers. They both decided they were going to give theirs to an elderly man in the church. This bothered me, I didn't understand this. Didn't they love their mother, and why give it to a man?

"Why aren't you giving this to your mom?" I asked. They told me they like the man better because he gave them candy. Ok, that was a little different but it got me to thinking and my imagination to running. Put that together with the fact I was still thinking about the dead turtle and my mind really took off. What if I died like that turtle had, I would want my mom to have these flowers or otherwise she would never get them and never know how much I loved her - things I really wanted her to know.

Pastoring a church of any size has unique demands on spouses. (Almost exclusively women in those days). I think this is especially true of those that take on churches with smaller established congregations. The expectations a church family has of its pastor can be demanding, but are equally as difficult for the pastor's spouse. They are often held to a standard that is not only higher than those expecting it, but quite frankly, unreasonable. Often those who expect these high expectations are unwilling to live up to them themselves.

FOR WHAT IT'S WORTH

Pastors' spouses share in the burden of the ministry.

- Your spouse is included in what you do whether you like it or not.
- Your ministry is for Christ and it begins with nurturing the spiritual health of your spouse.
- The spouse of a pastor encourages their husband by the power of their influence, just as the pastor encourages their spouse by the power of his influence.
- In addition to the ministry, the spouse often leads or participates in many ministries in the church.
- You must take time away from the influence of the church together on occasion, so that you can better serve one another.

"But encourage one another daily, as long as it is called "Today," so that none of you may be hardened by sin's deceitfulness." Hebrews 3:13

Popcorn and Girl Power

Fourth grade hit me like a ton of bricks, or rather I was hit with my teacher, Mrs. Anderson, and classmate Paula. At school, we had an enormous slide on the playground. It was the really high metal kind that would burn the flesh off your body on a hot day, but who cared, it was fast! Everyone loved it! I don't think you could find one today, they have probably all been removed, because someone screamed about how unsafe and what a health hazard it was. Yes, it was dangerous but we are still alive, even with the scars to prove it. For all us kids it was important. The lines to go down on it were huge, but it was especially significant to me because that's where I met Paula. Most of us went down the slide together in trains. You would put your legs around the person in front of you and zoom down like a rocket. Yeah, I know that wouldn't be allowed today either. At the bottom of the slide there would be a marvelous crash as everyone in the train ended up in a big pile. It just so happened that I got to slide down in front of Paula. It was love at first flight. She was so reckless and her enthusiasm for the slide hooked me, along with thinking she was really pretty. I decided I was going to let her know just how I felt. After school I went and found my ring from the very rare Super Sugar Crisp box of cereal that we got, (it was usually Wheaties and Cheerios). I couldn't wait to get to school the next day to give it to her. I had it all planned out and knew just what to do. I was very romantic; I hid the ring in her popcorn bag when we had a movie at school. I kept waiting for her to find it and pull it out and put it on her finger. She seemed genuinely excited to wear it and gave me a big hug, but it didn't last long. She wore it for about three days and threw it at me on the playground when I told her that Mrs. Anderson was pretty. I couldn't believe it, just like that and it was over. I was devastated, a broken man, desperate for love, and I had blown it.

Fortunately, in my mind, Mrs. Anderson was still available, and I was going to do everything I could to make Mrs. Anderson happy. It wouldn't take long for me to mess that up too. I was in class working on an assignment when all of a sudden nature's call struck me, hit me hard, like it does most fourth grade boys that drink too much water at lunchtime, I had to go! And go bad! And go now! I raised my hand. I waved my arm. I squirmed in my chair. Finally, she called on me!

"Mrs. Anderson, I have to go to the bathroom." I pleaded.

"All you kids always have to go during class. Just wait." Mrs. Anderson, said.

I held it for as long as I could, but the floodgates finally burst open. My wooden seat was filled, it ran down the pipe holding the chair to my desk and created Lake Michigan right under my seat. I thought to myself, "what am I going to do?" Just then my "Ex," Paula raised her hand.

"Yes Paula," Mrs. Anderson said.

"What is that water under Larry's desk?" asked, Paula.

Strike one, I knew, Mrs. Anderson would never fall for a pants-wetter. I figured it was over before I even got a chance. However, she felt so badly that she took me home in her own car during lunch, so I could get cleaned up and changed. Hope sprang eternal, I just knew she must care if she would take me in her own car. I wasn't out yet. Unfortunately, the battle for Mrs. Anderson's affection took another swing and a miss when I was being disruptive in class. Back in those days collecting pencils with football team logos was a big thing and my friend and I got into an argument over which was best. For behavior such as this we got spankings in school. Real spankings, with a real paddle.

Today's parents would be horrified, and a law suit would be sure to follow. You were told you were going to get a spanking, how may swats, and why. Your teacher and the principal would escort you out into the hall, make you face toward the wall, and then administer the corporal punishment. I knew it was coming, and I had only a small window of time to prepare so when Mrs. Anderson was conferring with the principal, I slipped my textbook in my pants to help shield the blow. Sadly, my pants were a little baggy and the book shifted down one of my pant legs as I walked out of the classroom. I got three well-deserved and well-placed swats that day. I thought for sure my love life was over but it was just beginning.

My third strike came when we were standing in the hallway getting ready to go to recess. I was standing in line with a ball that I had checked out of the box in our classroom. I was hardly able to stand still with it, throwing it up and down, higher and higher. I was only doing this to try and impress Paula. The problem was I threw it a little too high, lost control and bounced it off the fire alarm switch on the wall. When the bell began ringing Mrs. Anderson's eyes found me standing there with a guilty look on my face. Strike three, my short-lived love life was over. Well, at least for the fourth grade.

FOR WHAT IT'S WORTH

Your kids are not perfect. Get over it.

- Even though there may be expectations for your kids by the church, they only need to meet yours.
- Punishment given without instruction and council is simply abuse.
- Discipline given too much or too little produces rebellion. Different personalities require different approaches, learn what's best for your own kids and use them.
- Your children are your first and most important disciples. God has entrusted them to your care to help them know Jesus authentically.

"Foolishness is bound up in the heart of a child; The rod of discipline will remove it far from him." Proverbs 22:15

Paper Routes and a 1979 Selfie

"Larry, get up! The papers are here, and you've got to get them delivered." Mom would often say this to me at 5:00 a.m. on Sunday mornings. No, it is not child abuse. I would crawl out of bed moaning and groaning. Who knew 5 a.m. was soooo early? After getting the papers ready and loaded in the carrier bag I would sling it around the handle bars, hop on my bike and off I'd go. (No helmet needed, a shocker, right?) Sunday was the hardest day of my week. The rest of the week was easy, because the papers came after school and I could walk around in our little neighborhood and be home in plenty of time to challenge Dad to another game of chess. We played a lot of chess, at least until I started beating him, which was probably because he was exhausted from work and I learned to capitalize on that fact.

Five o'clock in the MORNING was way too early for this nine-year-old to get up on Sundays. I learned at this early age that getting up is where the money is, the early bird does get the worm, I mean money. Mom handled the money. She would keep track of the papers delivered and if a day was missed. One week I was anticipating getting paid and couldn't wait to get my pay, but there wasn't twelve dollars, like I expected. There were only eight.

"Mom? Where's the rest of my money?"

"Remember when you didn't get up and deliver your newspapers? Well I did, so, I paid me."

She was right, of course. It wasn't the last time I had to learn that lesson. When I was a teenager, I had an after-school job mowing lawns. I once asked her to take the lawn mower to one of my jobs after school, and she agreed. I was planning on meeting her there and doing the job. However, instead of going right to the job, I went to the arcade with my friends and goofed around for a while, taking my time to get to the mowing job. When I arrived, the lawn was already mowed and the five dollars that went with it was in Mom's pocket. Once again, I was reminded the one who shows up gets paid up.

That wasn't the only lesson I learned, I also learned that not only do you show up but you pay attention or the unexpected could take you out.

One of Mom's pastimes was playing on the church softball team. She really enjoyed it and took it seriously while having fun. Mom would gather us up and take us all to the field across the street to help her practice. I would pitch to her so she could practice her batting! Amy played outfield and chased the ball and Danny was his carefree, little blonde self, running around chasing butterflies, not caring what was going on around him. It was in this field that I learned pitching is dangerous. Pitch after pitch Mom would hit the ball, which was surprising considering I was an awful pitcher. This one time though, I managed to throw a perfect pitch and she hit it, connecting with it perfectly. It was a solid line-drive aimed straight at my head. That thing must have connected with my head because the next thing I knew, I was going down, tears flowing, pain radiating and a big knot on my head. Quick as could be we left that field and went home. I was set down at the dining room table and given a bag of frozen vegetables to hold on my throbbing bump.

I learned a lot of lessons in this neighborhood, along with having a lot of fun and adventures.

I think our neighborhoods were pretty cool when I was growing up. Before cell phones and the internet we were sent outside to play and find adventures in our own neighborhood. We rode bikes, ran through the cornfields, collected fireflies and played in the dirt and made friends with the other kids in the neighborhood. My siblings and I all learned really quickly that if you told Mom you were bored you were told to go outside or handed a broom. There's no choice between going outside to play and explore or cleaning.

One day, Mom loaded us kids up and we went to the store to get some film developed. Dad really loved photography and was a big

picture taker. It seemed as though we were frequently going to drop off film for developing or picking up the pictures that were printed. Our whole family loved taking pictures or posing for them. We thought it was fun to go along to the store to drop off the film or pick up the pictures and get to look through them. We waited in the car while mom went in to drop off the film and hoped there were more prints to pick up. Mom hopped in and started going through the photos. We couldn't wait for her to show us and let us see the masterpieces we knew had to be in there. Then with no warning, I witnessed something that I've only heard come out of Mom a few times, uproarious laughter that just couldn't be contained. I'd seen her laugh before, but this was of epic proportions, awe inspiring monumental merriment. This was the laugh of laughs. It was massive in volume, and so pure and from the soul that it caused tears like a river to flow down her face and her chest, heaving just to catch her next breath. When we asked her to show us the picture, she just couldn't seem to part with it, she was holding it so tightly to her chest. When Amy and I were finally able to get the picture from her, we saw what was so justifiably hilarious. Our little brother had gotten hold of Dad's camera and taken a selfie. Not just any selfie, but one with a look of extreme curiosity with a huge dash of, "I know I shouldn't have this camera, but I do."

I see now that things were difficult for our family back then. We faced some real challenges. Dad was between churches, money was tight, and we were far away from family. In the toughest of times never forget to laugh - alone and together. It will be the good times and the laughter that you remember the most and will keep you going through the toughest of times.

FOR WHAT IT'S WORTH

When times are hard, money is scarce,
and life is tough, just laugh.

- Sometimes you can't take this life too seriously, after all it's nothing compared to eternity.
- Delight in the people God has given you. They are worth more than all the wealth in the world.
- Don't be surprised when you face hard times. They will come.
- Rejoice in the Lord when difficulty strikes. He has permitted it so that your real joy will shine through.

"A joyful heart is good medicine,
but a crushed spirit dries up the bones."
Proverbs 17:22

"Anyone can kick down a barn, but it takes a good carpenter to build one."

Spinning Cars and Change of Plans

Dad was a multi-talented man. He and all his brothers were skilled carpenters and competent mechanics. He played multiple instruments and could make anything out of next to nothing. As a youngster I really didn't know what success meant. It was during those years when I began to compare Dad's secular employment to the work of being a pastor. The ministry, at least in my eyes, was lacking. There was a lot more money and time when he worked outside of the church. I started to believe that life was unfair (which it is), but more damaging, I began to compare and form judgements about which was better, and which offered more. Was ministry worth all these moves, all these sacrifices?

Mom and Dad heard about some of the needs in Montana for pastors and church planters, so we decided to move again. Dad had a couple of axels from a mobile home company where he worked for a while, and used them to build a tandem-axel trailer. It looked like most things Dad built, finished and professional; not a makeshift rig with worn out wheels and left-overs nailed together with the help of duct tape and bailing wire. This was a masterpiece with rounded fenders, shiny painted metal siding and matching wheel covers. We loaded all of our stuff in the trailer and hooked it to the Gran Torino. With Ohio in the rear-view-mirror, we headed to Montana. We were so excited; this was like a new adventure; Dad was going to be a Pastor again!

As Dad drove late into the night, I woke up to a bright flashing arrow from a road construction project as our car careened from side to side. The car began swerving all over the road. It was out of control as though it had a mind of its own and was rebelling. To make matters worse, we were on a bridge high over a valley! I held on to the front seat behind Dad as the car began a 180-degree turn. With his back arched, arms fully extended, and his hands clenching the wheel he shouted, "Praise the Lord!" The car and trailer skidded across the bridge, coming to a stop at the other end. We sat in the car as Dad got out to examine the scene. The entire rig had spun around, and ended at the other end of the bridge pointed in the opposite direction. In fact, it was so precise, that when the police finally arrived, they asked Dad if he was going the other way to begin with. To Dad it seemed like a tragedy, both axels on the trailer were broken and we were stuck sitting in our green Gran Torino on the side of the road with all our stuff in a broken trailer. I still believe it was a miracle we didn't go over the side.

We rented a truck and instead of continuing on we hobbled back home to Twin Lake, Michigan, to regroup and be with family. I loved going to Twin Lake, home to both sets of grandparents, many aunts and uncles, and a bazillion cousins. Dad seemed disheartened during that time, but I loved this time of going home. Once again, we were with family, and there was nothing better to me than having loved ones around and cousins to play with. Dad went to work again for a short time and rebuilt a new trailer. One of Dad's brothers owned a duplex. We lived there nearly a year before making another attempt to move west to Montana.

At this point in my young life, being around our family and having money seemed much better than going to some church where I didn't know anyone. My young mind was just beginning to make comparisons to being a pastor or doing almost anything else. I recognized the security, acceptance and love of being with family and noticed a difference compared to being in vocational ministry. I know now that these are not fair comparisons because Mom and Dad were not called to do what was easy, but rather what was necessary.

FOR WHAT IT'S WORTH

God's purposes are always accomplished no matter what your plans are.

- Don't be surprised if and when God changes your direction away from where you thought you were supposed to go. He is equally as concerned about doing something in you as He is doing something through you.
- God will always act in His best interest for your life whether you behave correctly or not.
- God's purpose for your life is to grow in deeper relationship with Him and to serve Him with your time, talents and resources.
- We learn God's will through meditating on His Word, sincere prayer, and providence. Don't be discouraged by detours in the road, God has great purpose for your new direction.

"Many are the plans in a person's heart, but it is the LORD's purpose that prevails."
Proverbs 19:21

Fried Chicken & Grandma's Eyes

Grandma Shepherd, my Mom's mom, was a cook extraordinaire. Every Sunday after church there was a feast. It was one of the reasons that I was glad we weren't in Montana yet. Just thinking about it would cause my mouth to water and stomach to rumble in anticipation. Fried chicken, dumplings, and biscuits and gravy were staples. What else would you expect from a Southern Girl from Kentucky. Grandma was in the kitchen most of the afternoon, dishing out food from her own all-you-can-eat buffet. The whole meal was amazing, every dish a serving of love and comfort. I don't know how she did it all. She was very involved at church and still put out a spread that would put many five-star chefs to shame. Grandma was simply amazing!!

Both the Ellis and the Shepherd families were large. With both of them in the same town I had lots of aunts and uncles nearby, and cousins to play and goof around with. When I was little, my closest friends were all cousins. After church on Sunday, the small village of my mom's family would come over to eat and watch football with Grandpa. I spent a lot of time with Grandpa Shepherd; he was an interesting character. He was a living sports almanac and a huge sports fan. Grandpa kept Marlboro in business, I think he smoked more cigarettes than there are tobacco plants. I never saw him in church, but he was a pretty funny guy. All of the Shepherds seemed to laugh a lot. It was fun when mom's family got together, it was like a wave would hit and they would all be joking or laughing at something off the wall.

Grandma used to do a devotion most Sundays between Sunday School and church service. I was with one of my cousins one Sunday, as she was finishing up her devotion.

"Go back here," my cousin implored as we crawled behind the platform area of the church. Following his lead, we somehow worked our way under the stage. There was a vent in the front of the platform where we could look out and see all the other people in the sanctuary. We saw Grandma sitting in the second row then everyone stood and began singing. My cousin and I were laughing as we spied on the congregation watching each one and how they sang and worshiped. One of the great disadvantages at this point in my life was that I needed glasses, so everyone we were watching seemed just a bit fuzzy. My cousin, however, could see perfectly. His eyes and Grandma's eyes met on the third stanza of "Oh Lord Send the Power Just Now." He realized we had better make an escape while we could.

"Hurry, let's go! She saw us!"

We were busted. We scrambled out from under the stage and hurried into the service hoping to minimize the fallout. Grandma never said a word, acting as if nothing had happened - just life as usual. We had great anticipation around her the rest of the day just wondering when she was going to spill the beans to Mom. But she never did. That's just the way she was and one of the many reasons I loved her.

FOR WHAT IT'S WORTH

Transparency is a powerful quality if you have nothing to hide.

- Develop relationships with people that you can confide in. Respect them to hold you accountable, and be correctable.
- Admit when you are wrong and ask forgiveness sooner rather than later.
- Genuine apologies never include "but," "however," or "if I offended you..." Just say "I'm sorry, I was wrong" and leave it to the person to accept.
- The inability to apologize is a sign of immaturity. Don't get older without growing up.

"Nothing is covered up that will not be revealed, or hidden that will not be known."
Luke 12:2

Dump Trucks and Blown Transmissions

"Now let out the clutch slow and give it gas", Grandpa said as I drove the big red dump truck through the woods. I must have killed the thing a dozen times, but he kept on coaching. There is such a thrill to be in the driver's seat of a big truck, even if it was the stop-and-go jerking of learning to get the hang of the clutch. I loved the days spent with Grandpa. Not only did I get to learn to drive the big dump truck but he even took me out on his back-hoe, which wasn't as much fun because I had to sit in the back behind the cab in a box of chains. I didn't care though, as a kid it was awesome! I mean what kid doesn't like big tractors, right? My impression of Grandpa Ellis is one of amazement and curiosity. He seemed to know how to do just about everything and was willing to share the knowledge and experience. I wondered how one person could know so much. I wish I could ask him questions now that I was too young to even want to know at the time, from his experiences and ideas about theology. It seemed every time we spoke, the subject was always about Jesus, or he would sing while in the shop under some rig he was working on. I loved being with Grandpa and living in the same area where we could see them almost every day. There was nothing like going to Grandpa's house. The house they built was like most of the Ellis families in the area; new and neat, at least that's the impression of a ten-year-old. I thought it was odd that we would want to leave. Why even go to Montana and be a pastor again? Rural Michigan as a kid is where I wanted to stay.

Back at home, Dad and I were working on a project - a truck camper. Not a painted plywood shell like the one built by the backwoods brothers, but a real over the cab, full on, slide-in camper for a pickup. Dad had bought a brand new 1979 F-150, brown pickup with the 300-straight six, three speed manual transmission with granny-gear. It was beautiful. I remember so many details about the camper and building it, but the most memorable thing about it was getting it out of the garage and onto the truck. Dad built it to the max height the garage door would allow to get it out. He cut up broom handles and put them under it to roll it out. We didn't have camper jacks so we jacked it up a little at a time, as high as our bottle jack would go, putting whatever we could use for shims underneath before starting all over again. It was arduous! It was nearly high enough to clear the tailgate of the truck when one of the saw horses at the back, (where I was holding it), broke. The corner came crashing down trapping my leg underneath. Dad was able to lift it high enough to pull me out. I was none the worse for wear and surprisingly the camper suffered no damage. In fact, with the back lowered, Dad backed the pickup underneath the front, nearly half the distance, then with some muscle we were able to push it all the way forward.

With the camper secure on the truck we began loading it up. We were finally all packed and ready to go. We had the camper and a trailer loaded with all we had. We all climbed into the tuck and headed west. However, we didn't even get out of the state before the transmission blew. But it was only a few hours before Dad and Grandpa got it fixed. Grandpa and Uncle Ed bought a transmission for $75, drove out to where we were, pulled the truck over a ditch, and got to work replacing the blown-out transmission with the new one. The incident didn't seem to faze Mom and Dad at all, they maintained a great attitude through it all. Within a few hours we were on our way to Big Sky country. It was only the beginning of our westward journeys and the start of a new chapter.

FOR WHAT IT'S WORTH

Always keep the big picture in view

- Setbacks or pauses are only opportunities for God to work on the tools He is using to finish the big picture.
- Never get discouraged because of setbacks, it still doesn't change the goal.
- Encourage your spirit continually with God's promises, the big picture can only be painted one brush stroke at a time.
- Do your work and do it well, but don't get too comfortable because this life isn't it.

"For this slight momentary affliction is preparing for us an eternal weight of glory beyond all comparison, as we look not to the things that are seen but to the things that are unseen. For the things that are seen are transient, but the things that are unseen are eternal."
2 Corinthians 4:17-18

Road Trips and Sisters

"Where are we now?" Amy asked. I pointed to the RV table that was also a map of the United States. I said, "I think we are here because we just got to Minnesota." We would both look at the map tracing every mile along the way from Michigan to Montana. Dad and Mom rode in the pickup cab while Amy and I rode the entire trip in the camper. Yes, we rode in a pickup camper without seatbelts or helmets on and we are still alive. In 1980 we didn't have cell phones, we had CB radios. The window between the camper and truck didn't open so Dad had rigged up a speaker so they could talk to us. I have travelled over parts of South America, Mexico, Africa, and Cuba, but that trip was the most memorable. Riding in the camper gave Amy and I a lot of time to goof around and play games. We were (and still are) buddies, I wasn't the nicest of brothers but we always seemed to have fun no matter what was going on.

It seemed like road trips were destined to always be a part of my sister and my relationship. We have been on at least a hundred, but there was one I'll never forget, our road trip adventure to California. In 1986 I had just graduated high school when Amy and I decided we were going to make a quick trip from Seattle to Sacramento to visit our Aunt and Uncle. It was just a spur of the moment, no planning, and no permission, just go, kind of thing. After having dinner out with Mom and Dad, we just took off without a care in the world in my little Toyota pickup. We were excited, not really taking into account the distance or the time it would take. Realistically, eleven hours is conservative, but in our minds, it couldn't be more than six or seven? Naïve is in the dictionary. We left with a half-tank of gas, twenty bucks and the music cranked. We were partying! We ran out of gas just outside of Portland and put the twenty bucks in the tank. We stopped again in southern Oregon to get some food and gas. Without a credit card, and back then no debit card, we were stuck with a checkbook, which no one would take. I had a plan, "Amy, go over there and ask the gas guy if he'll take a check. You're a girl, he'll do it for you." She did, and it worked! Not only did we fill up, but he gave us ten bucks more, so we went to McDonalds and bought cheeseburgers. We got to Siskiyou Pass about ten miles from the California boarder when we hit a blizzard. Hungry again and tired and no way to make it further on a Saturday night in a blizzard with no cash, we crawled through on icy roads.

"Stop", Amy said, as she pointed to the side of the road. "See, they need help." A family was pulled over beside the road and had run out of gas. "Amy, we can't even make it ourselves, how are we supposed to help?" I said. He waved us down and we could see his wife and children in the back seat. He said, "Hey, could you take me to a gas station?" I said, "Sure". I had a canopy on the truck so Amy rode in the back while I drove nearly twenty miles before we got to a gas station. When we arrived, he said, "Hey, if you take me back, I'll give you fifty bucks." I said, "No problem". I've always been amazed at how Amy hears God's voice so beautifully and responds to the Holy Spirit's prompting. That was one night where my suspicions were confirmed. We were able to fill up, get food and make it to our aunt and uncle's house the next morning, really early. Uncle Bob was so gracious, and even gave us fifty bucks to get home. We had quite the adventure and learned quite the lesson.

Through all the adventures we have had the one thing I have seen and learned is to be willing to be a servant in any situation, just as Amy was when she listened to the Holy Spirit's prompting for that family. To be in ministry doesn't always mean being the pastor, it means being a servant.

FOR WHAT IT'S WORTH

Hearing and heeding God's voice should be a primary goal of every Christ-follower.

- Create environments where you can be alone to hear God speak to your heart through His word, by His Spirit, and through your circumstances.
- It is more important to hear God speaking than to tell Him how you're feeling.
- Put "God-language" (Bible, worship, Christian fellowship) in your ears and in view (of your eyes), and you will be able to recognize His voice over all the noise in the world.
- Hearing God's voice is the mark of being a true disciple. God is more interested in doing something in you as He is in doing something through you.

"Whoever is of God hears the words of God. The reason why you do not hear them is that you are not of God." John 8:47

Grizzly Bears and Girl Power 2

"He's out there", the ten-year-old-boy cried out as he slammed the door to the cabin. This was no manufactured story either, his tears and genuine look of terror was validation enough for me. We all rushed to the window as our cabin counselor consoled the boy. "There he is!" I said, as the enormous grizzly bear sauntered through Hungry Horse Camp in Montana. Several other boys rushed to the window to look outside. It was my first camp experience and it started off with a bang, literally. We watched as a man came out of the back of the chapel with a gun and shot it in the air, sending the bear running off into the woods. Our gun toting rescuer came to check on us. "Is everyone all right?" he asked? "Everyone's ok", our counselor replied. "That bear wanders through camp every once in a while, just don't go out of your cabin after dark, it'll be ok," our rescuer informed us. "Wander through camp," "don't go out after dark," with these thoughts running though our minds, we all went to bed that night, but I don't think I slept at all. I'm not sure any of us did. I didn't know it at the time but the bear would not be the thing that would keep me awake the rest of that week, but rather a girl.

The next morning, we had breakfast and made our way to chapel when I saw her, Sharyl. She was a pastor's daughter from a church just across Billings from where we were living at the time. "Everyone sit down, we're going to get started", announced the counselor. The first thing we did that Tuesday morning was to break up into teams for our games all week, and wouldn't you know it, Sharyl was on my team. We ate meals together and wrote notes to each other, it was love at first sight. Every night I was awake thinking about her. Talk about Girl Power. The Thursday dinner was especially important because you dressed in your nicest clothes and invited a date. Why they ever did this at Christian camps is beyond me. Nonetheless, we went together and I held hands with a girl for the first time in my life. I was elated. The problem was that we were about to be interrupted by something that neither one of us could see coming.

Thursday night was the last night of camp and it was also the last chapel service we would have. During that service we sat together in groups with those in our cabins. Sharyl and I could still see each other but that focus soon changed as our attention was diverted. As the service went on the speaker was talking about being baptized with the Holy Spirit. I cannot tell you all the details, honestly, I don't remember them all. However, I was struck with wanting God to really touch me and I was hungry for it. The speaker asked if anyone wanted to pray and ask God for this gift, I was hesitant at first until I saw Sharyl at the front with a group of girls with her hands raised and crying intensely. I was so compelled; I practically ran to the altar.

The experience was novel, I had been in church since I was born, I knew all the songs by heart, I could quote all the relevant scriptures for salvation, and I could beat anyone at "Swords-Up", (A game we would play in Sunday School to see who could find a scripture the fastest). But this was different, I felt something, it was heavy but refreshing at the same time. I was crushed but overjoyed, and the sensation, though hard to describe, was simply my spirit and body responding to God, crying out to Him for His touch. It was like my entire being was a water hose under pressure that needed to be released, so I released it. Needless to say, I was impacted by the Holy Spirit and have genuinely never been the same. And I know this sounds a little weird, but my interest in Sharyl changed as well, I saw her more as a sister than as a girlfriend.

I have never missed going to camp since, and now I'm fifty. Although there are many activities at camp like canoeing, hiking, and swimming, the best of my experiences was always spiritual. The chapel services, prayer times, and worship were the most meaningful for me. For the most part my experiences have been spiritually genuine and often intense interactions with God. I gained an incredible appetite for the Bible and memorized large portions of scripture, and I still do to this day. I have often wondered how so many people have never experienced God's presence. God gave me an insatiable desire for more and real fulfillment.

FOR WHAT IT'S WORTH

Be baptized in the Holy Spirit.

- Knowing you belong to Christ theologically is important. We have spiritual experiences with God that are very significant for shaping our life and ministry.
- Jesus said that we will receive 'power' when He baptizes us with His Spirit. Power for life, power to live for Christ, and power to tell the world about His grace.
- Spiritual experiences with God create genuine desire to grow deeper roots that produce better fruit.

> "...Did you receive the Holy Spirit when you believed?" And they said, "No, we have not even heard that there is a Holy Spirit." ... And when Paul had laid his hands on them, the Holy Spirit came on them, and they began speaking in tongues and prophesying."
> Acts 19:2-6

"He who works with his hands and his head and his heart is an artist."
Francis of Assisi

Guns, Porcupine Cuisine and Fried Rabbit

"Now, just squeeze it." Telling an eleven-year-old to just squeeze the trigger of a twelve-gage goose gun is more nerve-wracking than a long-tailed-cat in a room filled with rocking chairs. I was terrified, I had all kinds of thoughts,

"Will it hurt?"

"It's so loud, will I go deaf?"

"What if it knocks me over?"

With my finger poised over the trigger and all these thoughts running through my mind, I took a breath and squeezed.

BANG!

I'D DONE IT! It only took once and I was hooked, I loved guns! I couldn't wait to go out and do it again, to practice my shot over and over. What else would a kid living in Montana's backcountry do anyway? At that time you could get your hunting license at eleven with the passing of a safety course.

I think Dad and I went hunting every year we lived in Montana. It was so fun. The first year I had to use the twelve-gauge shotgun, but after that I used a thirty-thirty rifle. It was on Christmas that I got my very own multi-pump air rifle and I shot it all the time. It would shoot over eight-hundred feet-per-second, which was powerful back then, still is actually. I spent so many hours riding my bike to the dump, (which was basically a hole in the ground), just to shoot any can, bottle, or anything else worthy of my marksmanship. The school even had shooting during PE and hunter safety classes that we were all required to take as pre-junior high students. Having a gun, shooting practice and safe hunting were as natural as breathing. I couldn't imagine my childhood without it.

It's hard for me to imagine that people are afraid of guns. To me they just don't really know what they are talking about. Perhaps they are afraid because they have never used one or are concerned that they will be abused. I'm afraid of asparagus, but I know better than to ban it, and just because some people abuse something doesn't mean it should be outlawed or banned from those who don't abuse it. Alcohol abuse in America is responsible for more than quadruple the gun homicides and heart disease is the leading cause of death in America. That being the case, we should outlaw or restrict beer and chocolate before we put any conditions on guns. The Progressives should add that to their "Green" initiatives, I'm sure it causes global warming or something…

In seventh grade I had a friend that convinced me to go with him to a cow pasture and shoot gophers after school. The rancher liked us going there because it helped rid the pasture of the pesky gophers. Cows would step in a gopher hole from time to time and actually break a leg. We got to the field and there were gophers everywhere, literally by the hundreds darting here and there. My friend showed me the best way to bag gophers. The trick is when you see one go into a hole, you sit in a good spot and wait, he will eventually stick his head out and when he does then you take it off. I was hooked. We were shooting gophers by the dozens constantly. We shot more animals than PETA has protestors. Soon I had several guns, and went out shooting gophers anytime I could. My arsenal was so exhaustive it would give any Liberal a heart attack. And yes, I was a kid and I shot stuff, and have been shot by air rifles, without a helmet, and I still have both eyes, and am still alive.

We had a family in our church that was very poor. They invited us over for dinner and I'll never forget the lower level of their house had a dirt floor. That really struck me as a kid because I knew we didn't have much, but when I was with them I felt rich. One day this family's dad was working out of town and shot a porcupine, so that's what they served to us for dinner that night. I sat at the kid's table with Amy and their children and we combined our savory delight and put it in a potted plant next to the table when no one was looking.

That summer my dad's oldest brother and family came to visit with my cousin Rick. I took him out shooting and we saw these rabbits running all over the place. "We should shoot the rabbits", Rick said. "I've never shot a rabbit", I replied. (I think it's funny that we don't have as much an issue shooting cute animals as we do killing the ugly ones). We were able to bag two rabbits, so we brought them home to show off. Once my aunt saw that we had killed two rabbits and brought them home, she made us gut them, skin them, and clean them. She then fried them up and made us eat them. I've never had rabbit since, or hunted for something I did not intend to eat, but I was a great marksman. The experience of preparing them to eat was more than I wanted to ever do again.

FOR WHAT IT'S WORTH

You must have the quality of contentment.

- People who are not content should not seek vocational ministry. You are at the whim and desire of God. He is your provider. He is enough.
- Contentment requires seeking God. He will give you the desires of your heart but remember sometimes porcupine is salty.
- Enjoy the small things, laugh at the trials, and rejoice when God provides, even if it's porcupine and rabbit. One day you will feast on the best foods in heaven.

"Every moving thing that lives shall be food for you. And as I gave you the green plants, I give you everything."

Genesis 9:3

Burning Dads and Sliding Chihuahuas

"Do you want to drive?" Dad asked as we headed up the snowy road. It was hunting season and it was just Dad and I on this trip. When he told me we were going elk hunting, and we were going to camp out, in a tent, in western Montana, in early November, I was more excited than a Liberal getting a free cell phone. "Yes, I want to drive". Dad pulled over and got out as I slid over to the steering wheel. I was so excited, I knew one day this 62' Chevy Bel Air would be mine, with its 327 cubic inch V8 and two-speed-power-glide transmission. (Should have kept that car). Looking back, I wonder at Dad's sanity. The winding mountain roads with steep drop offs to one side were all hazards that I hadn't experienced before. Nonetheless, 'Dangerous Dad" gave me the wheel. It was enough to make any modern soccer mom lock the doors of her mini-van. I did just fine, thank you very much. We survived with no harrowing tales to tell.

We drove for what seemed like forever till we found a place to set up camp. It was so cold my nostrils stuck together if I breathed in too hard. We got the tent set up, built a fire, and roasted hot dogs. We had a Coleman heater for the tent and I am so glad we had it because it was cold! We finally went to bed and for some reason the heater quit working in the middle of the night. We woke up so cold I thought I would freeze to death. Dad worked on the heater trying to get it going

- all to no avail. We decided to start a fire, get warmed up and then try to get some sleep again before sunup and the hunting began. The fire was tough to start so Dad poured some of our fuel on the wood to get it going. He lit the match and started it up, but when he did, he leaned back and accidentally kicked over the fuel can and it splashed a line of fuel from the fire to his pants. I will never forget him jumping like a crazy person with fire dancing all around him as he stomped on the ground until it subsided. In the moment I couldn't decide if it was tragic or funny. The best part was that once everything settled down, he just started laughing. We survived the night, but were bested by the freezing cold and decided to go home without hunting.

Every winter we went ice fishing on Canyon Ferry Reservoir. It's a good size lake between Townsend and Helena, Montana. We would go early, cut our holes, set up our poles and hang out. I actually really loved it, and even though I don't care for fish, fishing was fun.

Dad and I were sitting on camping stools watching for our flags to move, when all of the sudden we hear this yapping bark of a dog. The people next to us had a shanty they had set up and the dog apparently had escaped his prison and was headed straight for us. I didn't know what to do except stand up and try to greet the dog. It was a Chihuahua with an attitude. He bit my pants and actually started to tear them; he wouldn't let go. Dad yelled at the shanty,

"Hey, your dog is out!"

There was no reply.

I could not get this dog loose. Dad pulled him, but he only tore my pants more. Dad backed up, his toxic masculinity was about to be unleashed as he measured the situation and lined up for the kick. The dog must have realized what was about to happen but it was too late for him. Dad caught him perfect and hard. He slid without any control gliding across the ice like a puck off the end of Wayne Gretzky's stick toward the goal, right into our furthest fishing hole in the ice. The poor little guy floundered in the hole and couldn't get out because it was so slippery. Dad quickly ran over pulled him out and wrapped him in his coat. The little dog settled right down and we made a friend that day. Dad always made our adventures fun and memorable.

I firmly believe that to be effective in ministry in the long haul, you must have fun outside of ministry work. All work and no play produce a boring life, like Mexican food without the spice. Hobbies and leisure activities are gifts from God to help relieve stress and lend the spice of life.

FOR WHAT IT'S WORTH

Do something - anything besides work all the time.

- All work and no play make you boring, unsatisfied, and no fun!
- Create time, make a plan, and carry out something that is not directly connected to your church.
- Learn to laugh at the small things, it will build up to much needed total hilarity.

"There is nothing better for a person than that he should eat and drink and find enjoyment in his toil. This also, I saw, is from the hand of God, for apart from him who can eat or who can have enjoyment?" Ecclesiastes 2:24-25

Noisy Kids and Superman

"Our vote is no, I'm sorry, thank you for trying out," said the lead board member of the church in Darby, Montana. Dad had applied to be the new pastor for an established church. We spent the weekend in Darby, just looking around and wondering what it would be like to live there, only to realize we wouldn't be staying. I don't know all of the reasons, but I do know one. Me. At least that's how I had felt afterward. Apparently, Amy and I had been too noisy during the service and the board members thought we were too disruptive or something. We were also the only children present. I can't imagine how Mom and Dad felt. Trying out to be a pastor of an established congregation in those days was hard and it still is today. Once they got your resume', along with many others, you were called for an interview and then you "tried out". Which means you preached on a Sunday morning, attended a pot luck in the afternoon to see if they liked you, then you preached again Sunday night and they would vote after the service. And in one day the entire congregation and leaders are supposed to know whether they liked you or not. I think the whole thing is crazy and unhealthy for the church and the candidate.

Finally, we left Billings and moved to a little town just outside Helena. Townsend was a beautiful place and I liked it. Mom and Dad planted another church there. An older couple, Bill and Margaret, had been asking the denominational leaders for a Pentecostal church in Townsend. We first met in Bill and Margarete's living room, Dad led some songs and had a Bible study. This went on for a while until we found a little place to rent just off the main street in town. It didn't take long before there were a few families attending and Dad had plans to build. And we did! We built a forty by sixty-foot building and it was awesome. Dad would work at Coast-to-Coast Hardware fixing lawn mowers and guns during the day, and we would work on the church building at night and on the weekends. This is what every twelve and thirteen-year-old-boy needs, driving nails, cutting sheetrock and hanging siding. I loved it. It's as if this kind of stuff was made for me. It was fun, it was physical and it was rewarding.

"Push it up! Get under it, stay to the side!" Dad shouted as we pushed the forty-foot scissor-trusses up off the ground. There were only three of us there when the trusses were delivered. They didn't bring a boom truck so we had to hoist them atop the ten-foot walls and "roll" them to the other end. If you've ever rolled trusses you know it takes strength and finesse. Dad was in the middle on top with me on one end and another guy on the other side. He would hook the truss with a rope and pull it up and we would grab each side and walk it about half way down and stack it up. With the dirt grade beside the foundation and the ten-foot framed walls it was about twelve to thirteen feet to the ground.

Of course, there were no harnesses or safety rails - we walked on top of the walls, that's just what you did. Yes, I was twelve years old and rolling trusses, without a helmet on, and I'm still alive today. I've always admired my dad for being dangerous and graciously masculine. When we were able to get all the trusses stacked up, there was just one left, the gable-end-truss. These trusses are different because they have more framing in them that is vertical and on center all the way across. They are heavier. Dad hooked it and pulled it up, I grabbed my end, but when the guy on the other side grabbed his, mine slipped out of my hand and the whole thing started to go. The problem was that Dad was caught in the middle. There was no way to go but down. Thinking about it now, it all seemed to go in slow motion. With nail bags on, Dad jumped, curled up and rolled. Dad really was amazing physically - six-foot-four-inches tall, trim, agile, strong, able to leap off buildings in a single bound. Superman of dads he was. It's because of him I was doing varying kinds of carpenter work from the time I was big enough to hold a hammer, and learned most of what I know about building and framing.

Over the years I have met several church-planting-pastors. They are a rare breed, talented, determined and beautifully rugged. They are a kind of people that have vision, build, and because of the call, transform communities. They are leaders who lead and don't let setbacks deter them. They press forward doing what is comfortable and sometimes uncomfortable; willing to think out of the box.

FOR WHAT IT'S WORTH

God builds the church; however, you will feel the burden of responsibility for it. Bear it well.

- Don't be surprised when rejection comes, not everyone is going to like you.
- You are the leader, lead. Press forward, especially when the circumstances say otherwise.
- You will be required to do things outside of your skill-set. Don't complain, just do it.
- Don't, "not do". People will follow leaders who, "do".
- You will feel the pressure to "succeed". Ignore those who measure from the outside and take your feelings to the cross.

"Besides everything else, I face daily the pressure of my concern for all the churches"
2 Corinthians 11:28

Blackfoot Basketball and Humiliation

"Hey Ellis, you should play," my friend Jeff said. I really didn't know much about basketball but I was tall for my age, skinny and lanky, nearly thirteen and in seventh grade.

It must have been tough for Mom back then because basketball required stuff like insurance, shoes, uniform fees, etc.; expenses above what our budget was prepared to cover. She helped me collect bottles and cans to get the refund so I could buy the right shoes. Now socks - that's another story. Like any boy my age, I went through shoes and socks like crazy. I was always outside running around, hunting gophers and shooting hoops. I had a friend who had an Atari and I was mesmerized by it. Those are the kinds of luxuries we didn't have. We did have a small black and white television that Dad put in his closet every summer so we would go play outside, (something I don't think my boys could even imagine). I don't know why but socks have always been a highly valued commodity and still are today. I always joke that with four other young men in the house my socks go into the laundry and I never see them again. However, as a young teenager I went through more socks than an average person. I wore one pair for practices, (we practiced twice a day, before school and after), and another pair for classes and home. The cycle started all over again the next day. Little did I know that my reputation in the world of junior high was about to be written in stone because of socks.

Kids can be cruel. My world to this point revolved around my sister Amy, my brother Dan, and Mom and Dad. I was entering a new domain now, the cruel and unrelenting world of "Junior-Highish-ness." It all started when I didn't have any gym socks for practice for a few days. I honestly don't remember why. I think I had worn holes into ever one. It seems most likely that Mom probably threw them away and just hadn't had time to get any more. So, I had to wear some of Dad's black socks to practice. Not cool! This made me the laughingstock of my peers, even my coach asked if I had any other socks. For an entire week after practice I would pull off those sweaty black socks and head into the showers. What I didn't notice at first, (that everyone else did), was that the sweat had made the socks bleed and turn my feet black. I carried the reputation of "Black-Foot-Ellis" my entire seventh grade experience, from everyone - team mates, friends, rivals and especially the snobby girls. For the first time in my life I was categorized as the "poor" kid. I really didn't understand what it meant at first. I didn't "feel", poor. Nonetheless I was teased more than I would like to admit and it made me angrier than an atheist at a Southern Baptist Convention.

Because of the teasing and a growing awareness of why, I had a growing bitterness toward the ministry and the church. I knew the ministry was so important to Dad, I just couldn't understand why we had to do it and suffer for it. I told myself that if we weren't doing this, we'd have money for socks like normal kids and I wouldn't have to collect bottles to buy basketball shoes. The resentment and bitterness continued to grow. Why did we have to do this anyway? Why isn't the ministry "successful" so that we could have more stuff like everyone else? Jr. High is a tough time for most kids, but all these feelings made it even more so for me. I felt conflicted most of the time. I would have tremendous experiences with God and loved the Bible but my animosity toward the ministry was being fueled by my growing bitterness toward the church.

FOR WHAT IT'S WORTH

Ministry can be the worst place for peer-pressure.

- Never assume that the success of others is your rebuke. They are bearing their own burdens.
- There will be people that judge you and reject you. Get over it.
- Rejoice when others succeed. You will gain many friends.
- Find ways to encourage your peers, especially if you feel that they are more talented, creative, or smarter than you.
- Learn to let the snide remarks go. Only God's opinion matters.

"But I say to you who hear, love your enemies, do good to those who hate you, bless those who curse you,
pray for those who abuse you."
Luke 6:27, 28

Big Bikes and Sister's Scars

My twenty-inch Schwinn dirt bike with a banana seat, and sissy bars, was the coolest bike anyone could have. I also had a ten-speed, but because it was too big for Amy to ride, she rode my Schwinn to the crest of the enormous gravel covered slope. With the day's challenge laid out in front of us and my partners beside me, I decided the only way to get down this steep hill was to trade bikes. That way I could take Dan down on the Schwinn and Amy could take the big bike down that steep hill. Did I mention that this was a gravel road with a fortuitous slope? Yes, we rode bikes down dangerous hills, over homemade jumps, and through ditches with no helmets, and we are still alive with the scars to prove it.

Being the oldest and of course the bravest of us all, I would go down first. I had Danny sit on the front of the banana seat with his feet and hands on the handlebars. Pedaling for all I was worth we flew down the hill leaving a cloud of dust in our wake. "Ok, we're down, it's your turn", I shouted to my little sister as we waited around the corner just out of sight. All was quiet, as we waited for our sister to join us. Suddenly Amy's screams echoed throughout the canyon. As fast as we could we hurried back only to find that my little sister had lost control and paved the gravel road with her face. It was HORRIBLE! OH, THE BLOOD! It was TERRIBLE! The blood covered her face and was profusely dripping everywhere. At first, I thought one of her eyeballs was hanging out, but it was only skin from her forehead that had been filled with gravel, but because of all the blood it looked as though her face was falling off.

What were we going to do? We had to get to Mom and Dad, but town was about a mile away. Danny was able to ride the big bike, barely reaching the pedals with his toes while I put Amy on the handlebars of the Schwinn and started riding toward town. The backroads of Townsend were all gravel, it was constant bumps and Amy was crying inconsolably. We heard a truck coming behind us, "Amy, look at them when they go by, maybe they'll stop and give us a ride". Amy turned her bloodied and torn face toward the truck and looked right at them, of course they stopped, and stopped quickly. We threw our bikes in the back and they took us directly to the clinic in town. I can still remember sitting in the waiting area cringing every time my poor sister screamed as they pulled gravel from her face. Amy survived and remained my partner in adventure even after all the trauma and pain. From time to time she will lift the front bangs of her hair and show me the scar.

To this day she remains my partner in the adventure of ministry. Partners in ministry are invaluable. Amy has helped Pam and I since the very beginning of our ministry as senior pastors. Taking care of our kids, teaching classes and helping in just about every way possible, she has joined us as a partner, showing the strength of her love and dedication not only to her family but to God, as well. She is now on our staff leading a small army of children's and women's ministry volunteers.

FOR WHAT IT'S WORTH

The bonds of love are strengthened through tragedy.

- Never allow unforgiveness to divide you from your siblings or close friends. Life is wasted when we constantly expend bitterness.
- Never take up an offense on behalf of your loved ones. Two bitter people only amplifies the problem.
- Never show more grace to those you barely know over those closest to you.
- Your church is full of people watching how you love those closest to you. Be an example.

"The way we know we've been transferred from death to life is that we love our brothers and sisters. Anyone who doesn't love is as good as dead." 1 John 3:14

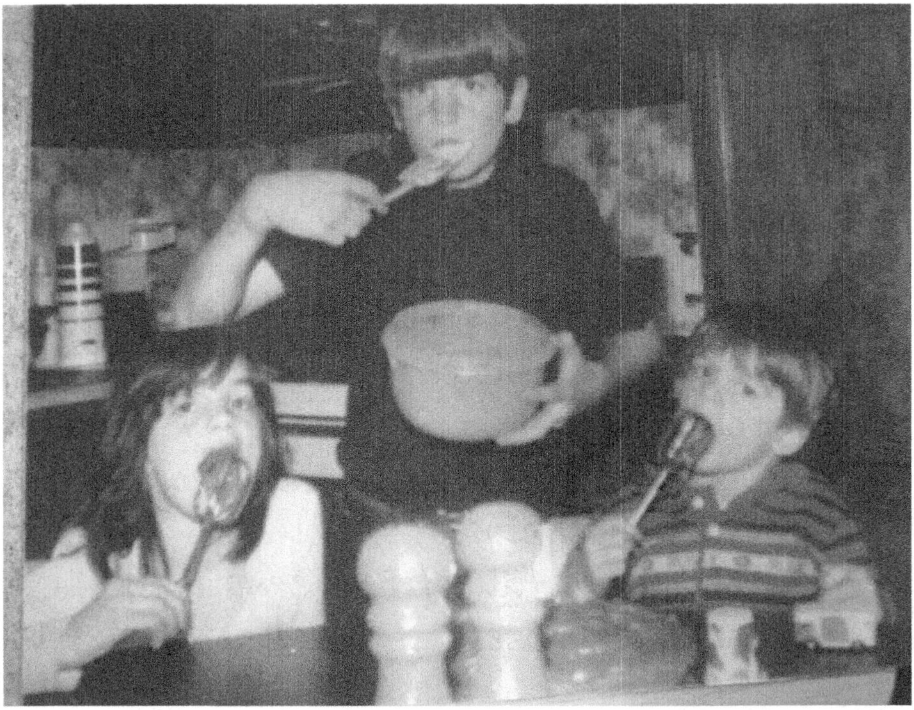

Brass Has Class

"A... L... X? P? Z..." I struggled to read the letters on the poster in the optometrist's office. Mom quickly noticed something wasn't right when I got into seventh grade. My homework piled up and I wasn't getting things done. She realized I couldn't see the chalkboard in the classroom. I'm just grateful I didn't shoot anybody mistaking them for a prize elk in the distance at that point. Struggling with that eye chart, it was very clear I was going to need help. So, I got glasses. It was a revelation! It was transformative! I had never realized how much I was missing. I had been able to bluff my way through things well enough to get by with squinting, up until this point, but junior high was more demanding. With my new glasses, my grades started improving and I could see things at a distance that I had never been able to clearly see before.

"Hey Ellis, you should go to the game with us tonight." Some guys from the junior high basketball team asked me to go to the high school varsity game. It was free for students so I went. My eyes were opened, not to basketball, but to the band. They had some dude playing trombone, standing at the top in the middle. He played so well, that I had never heard anything like it before. I had always wanted to play an instrument but they were always too expensive or we moved before I could get my bearings. As soon as I got home, I said, "Mom, I want to play trombone". She told me I should talk to the band teacher at school.

So, I did. It wasn't too long before they gave me an old trombone with a sticky slide to start playing, but since it was mid-term it was too late for me to join the band. The teacher was so gracious, he told me to come by after school and he would get me started. I couldn't get home. I quickly learned the fingerings for most of the brass instruments and couldn't put them down. I started playing the trombone in church and learning to play the songs by ear.

Finally, eighth grade started and I was enrolled in an actual band class; I couldn't wait! I soon realized I had a problem. I was way behind the music reading curve but way ahead in tone quality and range. If I heard it, I could play it. Trombone is the most obvious instrument for copying another. All you have to do is watch everyone else and move the slide like they do. I was a plagiarizing player. Townsend was a small school and the eighth graders played with the high school band - one band class for everyone. There was less than two hundred kids in the entire high school and about fifty in my eighth-grade class.

Mr. Aston said, "Alright, we are going to have a test in two weeks. You will be required to play the chromatic scale in two octaves and four of the major scales we have learned." I took it as a challenge.

There were four other trombone players I had to compete with. I was so nervous because I had only been playing for the summer, but some of these guys had been playing for years. Reading bass clef well was a learning curve for me and I had to ask what "chromatic" meant. I was behind. On top of all that, you had to play it in front of everybody as a solo for the whole band to hear! Even though the band was small, playing in front of these people was different than playing in church somehow. It was intimidating and nerve wracking but I wasn't going to quit.

    I went home determined to figure out the major scales by playing them on the piano. I listened to each note then played them on the horn till I figured out where they were on the slide. I was so slow at learning to read the bass clef music. Two weeks went by so fast, I rehearsed so many times I think my mom was going crazy. Finally, the day came and who gets called on to go first but the fifth chair newbie, me! I felt everyone looking at me and was more nervous than Hillary Clinton would be playing truth-or-dare. I started with low B-flat and headed up the range, past the first octave, throwing the slide out to fourth and on up cresting the high B-flat and back down again. After I got back to the bottom the class was silent, so I started my major scales, B-flat, nailed it, C, nailed it, E-flat, nailed it, F, nailed it. Just as I was hoping it was good enough, the entire class applauded. Mr. Aston said, "You realize you only had to do one octave on your chromatic scale." "No", I said, "I thought it was two." Mr. Aston put me at first chair that day over a senior, and I still struggled with reading music.

I believe my real love for music came from Mom and Dad. Mom really encouraged me during those years and I played and sang in competitions and won awards like many students do. I was given a talent and am glad I found it and was able to nurture it, and use it for the joy of others. I am blessed that music is a huge part of my ministry today.

FOR WHAT IT'S WORTH

God has given you talents and gifts, perfect them.

- Practice doesn't make perfect, perfect practice makes perfect. Excellence in anything is a powerful tool that God will use.
- Do small things well, I guarantee the big stuff will work itself out.
- Be a 'jack-of-all-trades', but master some.
- Never think success is having a lot of stuff going on. Small churches can have big impact when they do a few things with excellence.
- Follow the example of others that do what you do well. Higher education is not the only way to further your skill.

"But now bring me a musician." And when the musician played, the hand of the Lord came upon him." 2 Kings 3:15

"Measure Twice – Cut Once"

Bon Fires and Peppermint Schnapps

"Hey, why don't we all go camping?" Terry, one of my school friends asked. The four of us decided it would be a great idea and a ton of fun to go camping on the bank of the Missouri River just outside of town. (We all got permission from our parents, and believe me I don't know how we managed it.) However, four young teenagers were granted permission to go camping for two nights, on a small beach, by themselves, on the Missouri River with guns and fire, in the summertime. It was a recipe for disaster. Nevertheless, we did it and are all still alive.

The first night we decided we were going to build a big bonfire, better yet a floating bonfire. The Missouri is a pretty good size river and moves swiftly. To us it seemed perfect. We accumulated the biggest logs first and got them in the water, jammed them up with some rocks so they wouldn't float away and started to build. It was our Tower of Babel, rebellious, calculated and drenched in testosterone. The structure was so large that we had to climb up and hand smaller branches and sticks to the next person. It had to be ten feet high before we deemed it was ready. The wood was dry stacked and ready to be lit; it was going to be awesome. But once we thought about what we were actually doing we decided to wait until the next evening. A blaze that big would need attention and we were too tired to babysit all night. Smokey the Bear would not have been pleased.

The next morning, we ate our sandwiches and cookies for breakfast and proceeded to explore the riverfront. It was Sunday, and I was surprised that I didn't have to be in church, but Mom and Dad had let me go knowing I'd be missing church. My friend Steve and I shared a tent. He had a paper route early on Sunday morning, so he got up and rode his bike about four miles back to town, delivered his papers and was back before breakfast. I was very impressed with his dedication and drive. We had the whole day ahead of us and adventure was just waiting to be had. There was a lot to shoot at, fishing to be done, and that night a huge bonfire to ignite.

Later that afternoon things went sideways when Jamie's dad showed up with some alcohol for Terry and himself. Steve and I didn't want anything to do with it, but they drank and kept getting sillier and sillier. This was my first experience being around anyone drunk. I think the singing was the worst, perhaps next to the crazy story telling. I really gained some valuable wisdom that night. If you want to retain your dignity and valued inhibitions, don't drink. To this day, with the exception of peppermint schnapps, I've never even tasted any alcohol. I don't share Martin Luther's zeal for beer. That doesn't make me a prude or holier than others, it was just something that was never in my world and I genuinely don't see the purpose or need.

Jamie tricked me once at his house after I had come out of the bathroom. "Hey Ellis, let's have a guzzling race". Eager to please I said, "Ok". Needless to say, the glass wasn't filled with water, but rather peppermint schnapps. It never made it down my throat. How could something liquid burn like fire?! I thought my head would explode! I spit it out faster than a liberal can take your money. After all these years, I still don't understand alcohol and why people drink it. For the Christian who wants to follow Christ and be baptized with the Holy Spirit, there is no need. I realize the biblical context for alcohol and agree that drunkenness is sin but also that wine had a place and purpose in the culture. However, just because you can do something doesn't principally mean you should. It may be lawful for me to do, but it is not beneficial. I have seen it destroy so many lives, I just don't get it, anyway enough preaching; I digress.

Finally, time to light our Babel, so we lit the beast, it didn't take much. One piece of my lunch bag and one match started the beast. And it was a beast! The wood was so dry and the tower was fueling it so fast that we nearly lost control of the thing. I tried to move the large boulders out of the way hoping it would float out into the river and let the mighty Missouri extinguish the flames but the fire was too hot to get close enough. Jamie and Terry were no help, they were wasted. Steve and I could only stand back and watch hoping that we wouldn't burn down Montana. Fortunately, we were able to manage to contain the few out-of-control embers that popped out into the dry grass, and the fire stayed in the river and burned quickly. In fact, in about thirty minutes the mighty blaze had simmered down enough to where we could push it over into the water. To this day I am more than aware the dangers an out-of-control fire can cause. We were all very concerned about what may happen and were grateful that a catastrophe was averted. I am so glad that I didn't drink any alcohol, who knows what may have happened.

If it were not for baptism in the Holy Spirit and the fear of my father, I would have compromised my convictions that day. The fire of the Spirit on the inside was a greater force than any testosterone-fed bonfire.

FOR WHAT IT'S WORTH

Intervention is required to thwart the making of a rebel.

- Never think your kids are finished with you, because you are not finished with them. Teenagers require more nurturing than infants.
- Streaks of rebellion will come and go, but prolonged exposure produces reprobation.
- You have the responsibility to keep them in church no matter how they feel.
- Parenting never stops, it only transfers to a higher level.
- Biblical convictions in the home bear fruit outside of it. Setting Biblical standards that are contrary to culture guard the heart, protect the spirit, and ultimately cultivate freedom.

"All things are lawful for me," but not all things are helpful. "All things are lawful for me," but I will not be enslaved by anything." 1 Corinthians 6:12

Whiskey & Ginger and Girl Power 3

Every summer I would go to church camp in Montana. Each Fall I would go to school and lose my bearings. Youth camp always set me straight again. A re-establishing of my priorities. As a "tweener" or young teenager where your dad pastors the church is tough. If not for the trombone and singing, the church would have been difficult to bear. The problem is not what you would probably think, it wasn't the church, it wasn't the ministry, or the people. It was me. I struggled more and more with questions. "Why doesn't the church pay more so Mom and Dad don't have to work two and three jobs?" I kept wondering why Christians could not commit to giving to and loving their church. We did.

I had such genuine experiences with God, but my bitterness toward church and ministry grew. Dad and Mom joyfully and faithfully performed their ministry duties. I could not understand why they would take on this ministry when they could do almost anything else. I struggled the most against simple envy and jealousy. I wanted what everyone else had, without being burdened by the church; the liabilities of having to be in charge of everything, dealing with people issues, and money. I was young and did not understand what God's call to ministry meant. My parents were willing to give their lives, but I was not.

My questions met with more distractions. Girls rapidly climbed the list. I suppose once a young teenage boy discovers girls, he is forever changed. I had crushes on Heidi, April, and Shannon. Shannon was extra-special; we rode horses together almost every day after school. We corralled, saddled and rode horses in the backcountry of Montana without parental supervision. When we weren't riding, we hung out at her house, my house, the school and the church.

Shannon had two horses, Whiskey and Ginger. Riding horses was some of the most fun I've ever had. The mountains and hills on the outside of Townsend were an endless playground. We explored trails, raced through open fields, and pretty much went wherever we wanted to go. As a young teenager in Montana I learned to ride motorcycles, shoot well, and ride horses - staples for growing up in Montana. These were lifelines during that time in my life, I enjoyed them, but most of all I needed them.

However, once again my love-life shattered. Shannon's family decided to move to Helena. We never saw them again. I lost Shannon's friendship and a big part of my income. Shannon's dad offered to give us five dollars for every stray cat we brought him. As a mountain lion tracker and hunter's guide he used cats to train his dogs. I don't think I was the only one who felt the impact of them moving. I have often thought how discouraging and sad that may have been for Dad. The family was faithful members of the church and our good friends.

Ministry is built on relationships, in small churches even more so. When people bond and make life meaningful, the ministry becomes more effective. Perhaps this is the greatest reason God created the church. Sharing life's struggles and victories creates connections that are more important than money, social status, or popularity. When people move out of a small church it can be a tough loss for the pastor and the family, perhaps one of the toughest episodes they have to endure. People are valuable, relationships are rich, and possibly the singular item of worth on the planet you can take to heaven with you.

FOR WHAT IT'S WORTH

Choose your friends wisely, relationships direct life.

- Puppy love is not puppy love to the one smitten.
- Your future will resemble the future of those you have chosen to associate with.
- Good friends are necessary, without them life is boring.

"I thank my God in all my remembrance of you, always in every prayer of mine for you all making my prayer with joy, because of your partnership in the gospel from the first day until now."
Philippians 1:3-5

Noodles and Skunks

My eighth-grade year we moved into a house about a mile out of town across the highway from the rodeo grounds. That's when I met my best friend Kevin. He was a year behind me in school and his dad was the vice-principal of the high school. My dad continued to work at Coast-to-Coast Hardware store, fixing guns and lawn mowers. Dad continued building houses for a contractor in town to support his ministry habit. Kevin and I were thick as thieves. He called me "Ellis" and I called him "Noodles." I called him that because his last name was "Knodle." I thought about calling him "Needles" but it didn't fit him. We did everything two boys could do in Montana with guns, bikes, and a sense of adventure.

Behind our house sat a huge wheat field with massive stacks of hay bales. If you've ever seen ranch country you know what I'm talking about. Thousands of rectangular bales of hay stacked twenty bales high. The hay bale stacks are huge and fun to run around on. The one behind our house was no exception. We climbed all over that stack of hay bales, exploring every inch. Then we found it. The ideal secret hideaway. In the middle of the gargantuan mountain of hay, two of the stacks had fallen against each other at the top, leaving an opening at the bottom. It was perfect and we knew exactly what we wanted to use it for. We set out to bring our design to life. We cut down two small trees about six feet tall, shoring up the falling bales over the entrance, allowing us to safely crawl in. Once inside we had the perfect hideaway to store our stuff. And did we have stuff! Guns, ammo, flashlights, food, whatever you can think of to put in a secret hay bale cave. I mean what teen-age boy wouldn't want a hay bale cave for a secret place to stash all your worldly goods, right?

While hanging out in our perfect hideaway we heard something moving down one of the many crevasses. We had an idea of what it could be, but we were hoping we were wrong. It could be bad, really bad, if we were right. We shined our flashlights down a long opening and our suspicions were confirmed. There it was. A black creature with a white stripe down its body. We backed up. We grabbed our pellet guns, as any good sensible boys would do. Shot after shot we fired into the darkness, hoping to take the creature out before he could release his funk all over our perfect hideout. Unfortunately, the skunk had other plans. He wasn't in our domain; we were in his. Noodles, having taken the lead, was the recipient of the skunk's home security defenses. The smell was more than we could bear. Noodles was suffering, but the skunk wasn't finished with us yet. We had him cornered. Being cornered, he was in attack mode. He scurried out of his hole and came straight at us. With only my gun in hand, I turned around and made for the exit, Noodles right behind me. However, in my frantic exit I accidentally kicked out a tree holding up the entrance to the cavern, trapping Noodles inside. I could hear him screaming inside, but it sounded like Charlie Brown's teacher over the phone, or like Noodles had his hand over his mouth. I didn't need to hear the exact words, but I knew it wasn't virtuous or praiseworthy. I moved as fast as I could, throwing bales of hay in every direction to free my terrorized friend. After several minutes of frantically moving hay I was able to move a strategic bale enough for Noodles to squeeze his face out of the wreckage.

"Get me out!" I pulled his coat and got him free, but it was too late for Noodles. He received a full load of skunk spray. Unbearable. It's not like catching a whiff of a skunk while driving in your car. This smell was heavy enough to taste, it burned the hair out of your nostrils and brought tears to your eyes. Noodles' parents grounded him for a week and I lost a perfectly good flashlight and a pellet pistol. There was no way we were going back to get our stuff. It had become the spoils of the war. The skunk had won.

I stretched the boundaries of my liberties as a young teenager. I am so grateful for the experience of being a kid in the "Big Sky Country" of Montana. I believe there are many lessons you can learn far away from urban America and the incubators of craziness in many universities. After travelling to foreign countries, I realize how incredibly blessed we are as Americans. I am grateful to live in a free country, well free for now at least. These kinds of experiences and the values that go with them, are not as culturally accepted in America as they once was. The overwhelming ideology of our founders came from the Biblical principles of freedom. Churches carry this message and it must be preached.

FOR WHAT IT'S WORTH

Be grateful for freedom, it is expensive.

- Freedom in Christ paved the way for America's freedom. *"It is for freedom that Christ made us free..."* (Galatians 5:1b)
- Guard the freedom you have; it could be one generation from extinction.
- Freedom isn't only being free from bondage, but in really enjoying life.

God bless America, land that I love
Stand beside her and guide her
Through the night with the light from above

From the mountains to the prairies
To the oceans white with foam
God bless America, my home sweet home

Cow Tipping and a Jail Break

"Hey, do you want to camp out at my house?" I asked Noodles.

"Sure."

Once we cleared it with Noodles' dad, we set up a tent in our back yard, grabbed our guns, cards and food. However, our real plan was to sneak away after dark, head across the street to the rodeo grounds and shoot cows with our pellet guns. We proved two myths true that night: one, cow tipping is a real thing, and two, it's dangerous to carry guns in the dark.

Even in the summertime, Montana nights can be chilly. That night was cold. We snuck out of our tent, and made our way across the street. The rodeo grounds offered us so much fun as young teenagers. The tons of gates and fences became mazes for us to wander through. We had the run of the place, all to ourselves. The cows were in the pasture next to the rodeo. They would soon be at our mercy. We had heard a few friends at school say that cow tipping was real, but we didn't believe them. The idea says that cows sleep standing up. If you push them while they are sleeping, they will fall over. This is not easy to prove. It is difficult to find a cow actually sleeping at night time, at least it was for us. We thought we found one. However, when we got close, the cow walked away. It was proving difficult to find a sleeping one in the dark with nothing but flashlights. We didn't give up. It took a lot more time than we expected but we found one. At last! This time we weren't going to sneak up on it. We ran straight at it and gave it a good "Mean Joe Green" tackle. The rumor is true! You can tip a cow when it's sleeping! But, be warned. You stand a good chance of getting cow dung all over you. If you push too hard, he may roll over on you and almost kill you.

Noodles and I had made an art of sneaking out and adventuring. Once again, we were on the move. At the restaurant across the street, the last customer was pulling out of the parking lot. The car headlights shined on two men carrying rifles in the dark. As soon as the lights hit us, Noodles and I jumped down into a ditch and didn't move. The guy had a spotlight on his truck. We watched the beam shoot across the tops of the weeds lining the ditch.

"Be quiet, maybe he will leave soon." I said. I think we were more afraid of what our parents would do to us for sneaking out than what a random guy in a pickup truck may do. This guy didn't move. He must have had a CB radio because he called for backup. Backup that had red and blue lights on top of their cars.

"Ellis, what should we do? We need to get out of here!"

"I don't know." We were wearing dark clothes and I thought it would make it hard to see us.

"Just be still, maybe they won't see us."

That part of town had no streetlights, pitch dark. We laid still. Step after step the sheriff's deputy got closer and closer. He hopped over the top of the ditch, nearly stepping on Noodles when the terrified seventh-grader jumped up. With his gun still in his hand he began spilling his guts to the deputy, who also had his gun drawn. Noodles told the deputy everything he needed to know in about two seconds. Scared stiff and not wanting to move, I finally stood up and confirmed his story. The officers checked our pellet guns and told us to go home. What we didn't know at the time was that two men had escaped from the local jail. We learned the next day that men from the sheriff's office were looking for them that night. I have a high regard for law enforcement and the training they go through, and am grateful I didn't get shot that night!

FOR WHAT IT'S WORTH
Your experiences have taught you a lot, value them.

- Never trade common sense for anything, you earned it the hard way.
- It's always best to learn from someone who has tried and failed than from someone who has had it handed to them already done.
- Never stay down when knocked down, get up and keep on fighting. You have nothing to lose and everything to gain.
- Better to try and fail than never to try at all.

"For the righteous falls seven times and rises again, but the wicked stumble in times of calamity." (Prov 24:16)

"A man who carries a cat by the tail learns something he can learn in no other way."
Mark Twain

Pig Pens and Apple Fights

With a population of ninety-nine, Radersburg, Montana was a huge city. It's a little village about twenty-five miles from Townsend. When our family of five moved into town, we increased the population 5%. Radersburg was the first town in Montana we lived in and it would be the last town we lived in on our way out. I don't know all the details, but I remember the denominational group we belonged to sold the building my family built to pay for another building somewhere else. As a teenager it frustrated me not to have all the details, and I was hurt that something like that could ever happen. Didn't they realize how hard it was for Dad and Mom? Didn't they understand how tough it was on all of us? My bitterness toward the church grew as well toward Dad. I began to ask bigger questions with greater intensity, questions to myself about the value of being a pastor. I viewed the churches that Dad planted as part of his failures. I didn't appreciate that all of us stand on the shoulders of those who have gone before us. My parents were the shoulders for many of the churches where he ministered. My mom and dad are heroes.

Although Radersburg was small, there were more than a few kids there around my age and we were always running around. Three of these became my good friends and we hung out a lot together. Radersburg is a town of gold mines. The gold rush hit Radersburg hard.

There are literal holes in the ground all over the place. Once word got out about the gold, everyone grabbed a shovel and began digging holes, hoping to get rich. Our parents constantly told us to be careful when we went exploring, because people were known to have fallen into the mines. The mines were hard to see because grass and weeds had grown over the wooden covers.

Across the street from our house there were several apple trees. I soon learned that apples can be dangerous. Anytime there was a gathering of kids after school we would divide up into teams and have apple fights. An apple fight is the same thing as a snowball fight, except you throw apples. But if you ran out of apples you could use your BB gun, but you had to call out the switch to give people time to adjust. We all had to promise not to shoot at people's heads. BBs hurt! I've been shot many times with a BB gun and hit with apples, and I still have both eyes.

In such a sleepy little town, we were all kept busy. Mom worked for a wonderful lady cleaning house and a few other jobs. She must have thought my apple fights and BB gun wars were not enough activity for a young teenager. Mom decided it was time for me to have a job. She got me a job cleaning out pig pens for the same lady she worked for; clearly, I didn't have enough to do. When you're fourteen, shoveling pig pens isn't ideal work, but it paid well. It's not as easy as you would think. A couple of dangerous encounters with a big sow solidified my love for bacon.

Dad also worked on the lady's new home. I was his right-hand-man. This was the first time Dad had "The Talk" with me. I wish we'd had the discussion when I was closer to ten, but he cleared some things up. It wasn't an uncomfortable talk and he seemed genuinely concerned that I understood it. He explained that sex was for a husband and wife, because that's the way God made it. To this day it's difficult to not associate pig pens with "The Talk."

FOR WHAT IT'S WORTH

The influence of a godly father is powerful and needed.

- One day you will be old and there will be no more time to say what you needed to say, or act the way you should have acted. Do it now.
- Godly men in the home are counter-culture, expect to fight for what is right.
- Discipline your children with love and grace, never out of anger or disgust.
- Be unapologetically masculine. Your family and the world need strong gentlemen.

"Fathers, do not provoke your children to anger, but bring them up in the discipline and instruction of the Lord." Ephesians 6:4

Freshman and Fighting

"Excellent job, Larry."

"Thanks Mr. Arensmeyer," I said to my favorite teacher. At long last, I understood school. From the sixth grade to my freshman year I gradually improved, close to a straight A student. As a freshman, I played on the basketball team, (clumsily), excelled in band and choir, enjoyed shooting competitions, and I loved math. There were a lot of changes for me in high school. I built new friendships as I shifted from sports to being more involved with music and its different crowd with different interests.

I started to like school, but it was not without its challenges. Not the least of which were the fights I got into. I wasn't in reality living for God my freshman year. I would go to church camp and get all fired up. After camp, when I got around my friends and the everyday environment, I did whatever I wanted. I started down the slippery slope of concern for what my peers thought rather than what pleased God. The small church we attended had hardly any other young people in it. There weren't many opportunities to nurture spiritual sanity.

"You're a dumb @#&$!" I shouted at Bill. He insulted me in some way. I honestly don't remember how. It hardly matters. "Meet me behind the drug store at four-o-clock after school!" To my shame, I must say my temper would get the best of me during much of my early teenage life. I would lash out, get in fights, and was easily offended. I was pretty unafraid to get into a tussle with anyone; especially if I thought they were "snooty" or wore nice clothes. I learned that if you threw the first punch and landed it hard, in general the fight was over right there.

I fully intended to keep my promise to Bill. I headed straight to the drug store after school. Dad was walking downtown. He saw me across the street; the store where he worked was on the other side of the main street.

"Larry, where are you going?"

"I'm going to fight this kid behind the drug store."

My hope was that if Dad would somehow intervene, I wouldn't have to go through with it. However, he didn't say another word and kept walking.

I met Bill in front of the drug store.

"Let's get this over with." We started to walk down the sidewalk to the side of the building toward the alley when Dad showed up.

"Hey why don't you guys come down to the café and have a shake. I'll buy." I was delivered. Free.

Dad's conversation with Bill over a chocolate shake opened up a whole new world to me. Bill came from a rough home environment. After our milkshake encounter, I went to his house and saw the hell he lived. His dad was passed out on the couch, there were beer cans everywhere, and the house smelled like urine. Reluctantly, Bill let me come into his room. It was closer to a large closet with a mattress on the floor than a room. I knew we weren't rich, but Mom and Dad kept their dignity and standards no matter how tight things may have gotten. The experience of seeing Bill's home life affected my thinking. I began to appreciate the character of my parents and the things we did have, no matter how little of it there was.

When I wasn't lashing out and getting into fights, I had some lawn jobs that financed my video arcade career at Circle K and kept my vanilla coke fund supplied. After school I would go to either the soda shop or the arcade. I would hang out there and then ride home with Dad after he got off work.

The downtown had a little soda shop where Flo, and I'm serious, her name was Flo, would make me a vanilla coke. She was also the youth leader at the Baptist Church in town that we attended for a little while. Her input in my life is very valuable, she was a great influence. I would sit on a stool at the counter and simply talk to her. The youth group in the church was not much, but Flo's love for me helped through those transitional years. The activities she hosted were fun; but it was the long rides home that influenced me the most. She would listen to me rattle on about everything going on in my life and interject with laughter and genuine concern. She was a real friend.

The influence of church leaders on young people is monumental. I was directed in life by many people, some for good and some for bad. However, the adult Christians that took the time to talk to this rebellious teenager helped to chart my path. I know I would have gotten in a lot more trouble if it had not been for godly leaders speaking into my life.

FOR WHAT IT'S WORTH

Restrain your temper, nothing is worth losing it.

- Things are built during times of peace, fighting and war only destroy.
- When you feel you are losing your temper, control yourself! A text sent, a fist thrown or an unsavory word spoken can never be pulled back.
- Put better stuff in your environment. Spend more time in prayer and meditating on Scripture, God has better words.

*"A fool gives full vent to his spirit,
but a wise man quietly holds it back."*
Proverbs 29:11

Exploding Gas Cans and Screaming Moms

"Go ahead and light it, see what happens," one of my good friends, Jeff, encouraged me as I approached the bucket with gasoline in it. So, of course, I did just that, anticipating a great fiery explosion. The five-gallon bucket only had a little bit of gas in the bottom, but boy it erupted in big fiery flames then quickly burned out. "Oh, come on, that was it?" Not quite the explosion we were hoping for. I don't know what the fascination with blowing stuff up was for me then, but we were definitely fascinated with it and we blew up anything we could. We figured out that a well-placed fire cracker in a coffee can, upside down in a bigger can with water makes an awesome rocket. It took a while but we got our rocket flying down to a science with maximum height and the perfect flight trajectory.

We were risk takers and loved it, even when it didn't work out the way we wanted. I once had a firecracker explode in my hand next to my ear. I never did that again. And yes, I was a kid and played with matches and explosives without a helmet on and I'm still alive! I think if Mom knew half the stuff I did at that time, even after Dad was finished with me, I would still be grounded. Don't get me wrong, I had plenty of "wait till your father gets home" moments, but unfortunately, I also got away with quite a bit of stuff.

Jeff, however was not so fortunate. After I left our little gasoline bomb-making-session, he added a little more fuel to the bucket and he tried again. This time he lit it and wound up in the hospital with serious burns. I went to visit him and took a Rubik's cube as a gift - more of a peace offering and guilt gift. I was feeling guilty for his accident. For the longest time I threatened to call him 'butt-face', because they took some skin from his nether-region to graft onto his face. Fortunately, it was fairly minimal and he was none the worse for wear a couple months later. With Jeff in the hospital it was back to the usual stuff, you know like jumping over Amy on my bike, shooting spray paint cans, (awesome by the way), shooting stuff, and playing basketball.

At least playing basketball didn't get me into hot water and truth be told, I really loved shooting hoops even though I wasn't very good at it in those early teenage years. It took a long time for coordination to catch up with my lanky arms and legs and being so skinny didn't help any either. I took after my dad. My uncles told me once that if Dad were to turn sideways and stick out his tongue, he'd looked like a zipper; I suppose that could have been said for me also.

Mom really encouraged me while playing basketball. She loved going to the games, watching the action and her "gifted" son and seeing everyone she knew there. I had my own cheering section. Who would have thought that so much sound could come out of a little five-foot-short lady? She could put any 12th man to shame. She would yell, "Go Larry!", or I would hear her cheering when the team scored or did well. Looking back, I realize how influential Mom was by encouraging me to get involved even though at times I didn't feel like it and never really wanted to. I'm so grateful for my screaming mom and her cheerleading skills. Even when Dad couldn't be there she was there. She pitched in and picked up where he left off like a real partner in ministry especially when it was for her own family.

FOR WHAT IT'S WORTH

Cherish encouraging words from loved ones, not everyone has them.

- You will be affected by words. Culture flourishes on words of death - it is in entertainment, media, music, and people. You must counteract this impact with God's words of life.
- Never distance yourself from those who encourage you. God is speaking through them to give you hope.
- Always find ways to speak uplifting words to others, it has a way of coming back to you.

"It is not good that the man should be alone; I will make him a helper fit for him."
Genesis 2:18-19

Pump Organs and Ceiling Fans

In one of the churches where we were, there was a canvas covered lump just waiting to be explored. Dad and I pulled off that canvas which was covering an old pump organ. With a little time and elbow grease Dad soon got it up and running. Boy did that organ have volume, with the doors open that organ really echoed outside. Soon we started having church, and in the summer, boy did it get hot in that building; there was no air conditioning and the windows didn't open, in fact some were boarded up. There were ceiling fans but we had never turned them on. I remember one Sunday after everyone had come in, (our family, a Baptist family from Townsend, and a few others), Dad decided to try to do something about the heat. There were four ceiling fans all connected to an electric motor by a long belt which would run all of them at one time. Dad decided to turn them on. I think some people may have asked if he could, I don't really know. Anyway, he flipped the switch but nothing happened. He told me to come to the switch and turn it back on when he said to. He disappeared for a while trying to find out the fuse issue that was keeping the fans from working. He finally yelled out, "Larry, turn it on." Well, I did, and everything that had accumulated on top of those fan blades since before Moses - dust, dead flies and other bugs, all came raining down like snow on Christmas. I actually thought people would just leave, but they were actually quite accommodating and gracious; they just dusted themselves off, settled in and had church anyway. It wasn't all that funny at the time, but looking back now it is hilarious.

Ministry must have been interesting during that time for Dad. I have always been impressed with his ability to smile in spite of all that was happening - some of which, at least to me, seemed quite tragic or at the very least a big set-back. Planting churches is hard work when you are on your own. A real roller coaster ride to me, multiple ups and downs and setbacks that would make a weaker man throw in the towel. These days many have another supporting church that sends people and resources out to make it happen. Not with us, I felt we were genuinely on our own.

That feeling of being on our own caused my skepticism of the church and denominational leadership to grow despite my love for God. That skepticism and resentment continued to grow, becoming a real battle inside me. It was a quandary, because it is impossible to really love God and not love His bride. This is the blessing and burden of those who choose to answer God's call to the ministry. Loving the church brings the responsibility of taking care of it. Ministering the Word, managing resources and juggling people issues, all while working a full-time job to meet the needs of your family - boy, does it take a lot of work!

FOR WHAT IT'S WORTH

Personally, never compromise the Word and a healthy devotional life because:
- God is more concerned about you than your ministry. Your spiritual health is more important than what you are doing.
- Your first ministry is to the Lord, keep Him close, keep the relationship real, and keep Him first. He gets the best of everything.
- You cannot minister with power and authenticity if you are not living it. You may have a crowd without it but you will never have true ministry.

"And you shall love the Lord your God with all your heart and with all your soul and with all your mind and with all your strength." Mark 12:30

"God never said the journey would be easy, but He did say that the arrival would be worthwhile"

Big City Blues

Leaving Montana was tough for me, not for the reasons one might expect; surprisingly it was the teachers that I would miss the most, specifically the principle, and my math and band teachers. I asked Mr. Aston, band teacher, if I could buy a school band jacket and he said they were not for sale. My mom even asked if we could purchase one - I really wanted one but they told her no. I was called into the principal's office the day before we were moving and was wondering what was going on. The principle was standing beside his chair and began talking to me. He said, "Larry, you're a good student and I know how much you love band, so we can't let you go to Washington without a band jacket." He turned his chair around with my band jacket draped over it. "This is yours". I actually hugged him I was so moved. Even though at times I was hanging out with trouble-makers and making a bit of trouble myself, I really felt like I belonged. Living in a small town does have its advantages.

"You've got to help me stay awake", Dad said after driving all night. "I'll try", I said, "but I'm so tired." We were moving away from Montana, away from all my friends, away from basketball, and away from shooting stuff, at least that's what I thought. I did not want to move to Washington, someplace called 'Enumclaw'? I mean what good can come from a place that meant, "Home of the evil spirits"? That's like trying to get a conservative to move to California, I was not happy. Little did I know that God knew I needed Enumclaw, and more specifically He knew I needed church and the youth group I would encounter there.

Enumclaw is not a big city, in fact it's kind of a sleepy town just southeast of Seattle, right at the base of Mt. Rainier, and it's beautiful! Even though it was a small town it was huge compared to the environments I had been used to for the last several years. I think my sophomore class in Enumclaw was about three hundred forty students, while the entire high school in Townsend was maybe two hundred. To me this felt huge! A thousand students in high school, how is that even possible? It was a culture shock; I wasn't sure how I would adjust or if I could. Mom contacted the school and asked about the band program before we got there. They asked me to play in a parade that summer before school started; this gave me an early introduction to some of my would-be classmates.

Enumclaw was different in more ways than just being a lot bigger. We weren't leading the church anymore. Mom and Dad both had jobs, they started making money, and bought a house, and we began going out to restaurants, (I think because there were actually some around more so than for money reasons). This place seemed huge to me, a down right metropolis it was, and I would be in for quite a change; and I was deep into the big city blues.

Church is what got me through it all and made it for me, specifically the youth group. I walked in with my band jacket on into a circle of about a dozen teenagers. They all welcomed me like I was already one of them. That's where I met "her", a brunette with a huge smile. I didn't know it at the time, but Pam would steal my heart and become my wife. As part of the youth group we would sing some songs and then our youth leader, Pastor Tom, would speak. It was my first real experience being in a youth group. It was very genuine and would be the place I would really get my bearings; a place that would help ground me once again.

Youth ministry in a small church is vital. Young people really need to be part of the church today. It gives them stability and a place to get grounded, and more importantly, if they aren't, they will not be the leaders of the church in the future.

FOR WHAT IT'S WORTH
Change requires flexibility and requires us to grow in character.

- Be flexible to God's plans, they are after all, His. A person inflexible to God's ways will usually be flexible to bad ideas.
- The pain you experience when required to be flexible is directly measured against how much affection you have invested in this world.
- The more concerned you are with the cares of this life, the less you will understand flexibility.
- Your one life yielded to God at all cost will produce much more fruit than the many who are only touched by God.

"For where your treasure is, there will your heart be also."
Luke 12:34

"As a house implies a builder, and a garment a weaver, and a door a carpenter, so does the existence of the universe imply a Creator."

Luc de Clapiers

Jesus Freaks & Evolution

"But how did twenty-four-proteins get so complicated and able to make life?" my biology teacher would calmly ask as we studied the theory of evolution. I've always had more questions about evolution than Richard Dawkins has explanations for getting something from nothing. My teacher was gracious but didn't put up with it too long. I was certain that God created everything and for someone to say that something comes from nothing didn't make sense to me, still doesn't. I wouldn't answer the questions about evolution with the "facts" they wanted. I was soon kicked out of Evolutionary Biology and sent to Earth Science class, but not for questioning evolution and refusing to answer with the facts they wanted, but rather for making trouble.

I genuinely hated school in Enumclaw. I'm not at all being overdramatic, and to this day I wonder what redeeming qualities it had for me even though Band was probably the one positive there. With the exception of a few friends, this new school had several 'classes' of people, or 'cliques', and certainly wasn't the family environment school that I had come from. I didn't love the coaches, teachers or the principal. I got bad grades, I didn't want to participate, the cool kids were trying to get me in their club, the rednecks were trying to get me in their pickup trucks, and the stoners were trying to get me in their cult. I actually fit in best alone, with just a few friends. I honestly wanted to just be in band all day and play music or go to the gym and shoot hoops - not with a class or a team, just on my own. High school in Enumclaw really was like the 'Breakfast Club' on steroids for me.

I quickly found myself in trouble when my lab partner was snorting drugs off his biology book in the middle of class. By trouble, I sincerely mean, I didn't know what to do. I didn't know if I should rat him out or play along like nothing was happening. I have never tried drugs, and never wanted to but like him. I had many of the other misgivings and questions about life and purpose and trying to fill a void. I too had my own way of engaging in simple rebellion. When the teacher left the classroom, I turned the gas burner valves on and lit them so that little flames were shooting out each side of the four lab sinks. "Who did this?" my teacher demanded, as his forehead would curl and turn red. No one answered. He came back and turned them off, but I knew that he had me nailed. The next day I took a two-liter pop bottle with just the right proportions of crystal Drano, aluminum foil and water, shook it up and put it in my lab partner's backpack. It was a huge explosion that ripped a hole right in the side of his pack. "Who did this?" Once again, my teacher demanded to know, looking right at me. "Mr. Ellis, meet me in the teacher's room." It was a room between the two science classrooms where teachers would go to take a break. He calmly wrote a note and sent me to the office. The vice-principle simply told me to report to Earth Science class. I'm so ashamed of the way I behaved, and I so hated school. I was very hypocritical, taking my Bible to school to study for Bible Quiz, (a competition that required memorizing large portions of scripture), all the while behaving in ways that would shame the Lord and my parents.

It wouldn't take long however, for me to hear God's voice once again. The church was different; it kept me sane and began to give me a solid ground to get my footing. All the youth sat up front and worshipped, I mean really worshipped. They didn't hide in the back or sit out go out witnessing, prayed for long periods of time at the altars together, and shared a deep drive to see our schoolmates come to Christ. I genuinely witnessed others unapologetically sold out for Christ. For the first time I was in a group of young people that seemed serious about loving God, this was new and exciting and I was drawn in. Outside of camp I had never seen young people with such genuine love for God, for the Bible, and worship in church. My resentment however, for the years of struggling that Mom and Dad had endured, remained. I didn't want anything to do with ministry, I genuinely thought everything we had ever done was a failure. I was conflicted and torn. How could I be drawn to all of this and still want nothing to do with ministry?

The opposite seemed to be true for Dad, who never flinched. He jumped right into the church; teaching, serving on the Board and just supporting the pastor. It was how he lived and breathed and it was truly in his DNA to be that way. Looking back, I so admire him for that, it is inspiring.

FOR WHAT IT'S WORTH

God hasn't called you to simply be a sub-culture, He's empowered you to be unapologetically counter-culture.

- Put things in your environment that affirm your faith. The music you listen to, the movies you watch and the activities you do must nurture deeper relationship with God.
- Love God's church and be faithful to her.
- Be willing to stand alone when your convictions are pressured to be compromised.
- Standing alone should always be based on loving God, not reacting to people.

"Therefore, go out from their midst, and be separate from them, says the Lord, and touch no unclean thing; then I will welcome you,"
2 Corinthians 6:17

Camps and Calling

"Are you going to camp?" the youth pastor asked. "I hope so", I said. I was hoping that camp would be the same as I had always known. I loved the time spent around the altar; I still do. I was really impacted at camp when I was younger, but this was a new place with new people and I didn't know what to expect. That summer we all packed into the baby blue Dodge church van and headed to camp. One of the girls in the youth group, (Pam, my future bride), had given me a cassette tape of Russ Taff's, *Walls of Glass* album. I had been around music all my life in church; lots of Southern Gospel sounding stuff, but what I heard on that tape changed my world. Not only that, but there was a radio station that actually played this kind of music. Awesome! I didn't know that even existed. I knew there had to be something Christian that was better than Journey and AC/DC. My eyes were opened and I've never gone back. I wore that tape out until the cassette broke so I took it apart and put the tape in another cassette. I soon gravitated toward Steve Camp, Whiteheart, Petra, and the list goes on and on and on. My world exploded with music. Christian Rock saved me and I couldn't get enough. The van rocked with this stuff the whole way to camp and back.

We pulled into the driveway at Cedar Springs Camp; I was hesitant at first, wondering what kind of experience was waiting for me here. We got settled in and survived the first night. During the day we played all kinds of games, went swimming and played basketball during free time. If you've ever been to camp you know how it goes; they start on Monday with the message of salvation and work up to Thursday where you're seeking baptism with the Holy Spirit or filling out an application for Bible college. I was put off a bit at first because I went to the prayer time before the services and there was this guy who would pray really loud and then look around to see if anyone was watching him. He seemed like such a show boat - I wanted nothing to do with that. However, later in his life, God called him and he became a pastor of a large church.

It wasn't until Wednesday night that I began to really hear God speaking to me. It was an urgent appeal to say yes to ministry. I was so resistant; I hated the very idea of it, bitterness and resentment still sat heavy in my heart toward ministry. I had in my mind, categorized everything that my father had done in ministry as a failure and I didn't want to go down that road. The speaker at camp was from Redding, California. He spoke very prophetically as he looked over the crowd of high school students, one by one calling them to the altar simply to seek God. I was sitting there resistant to everything, I did not want to be a pastor, a preacher, missionary or whatever, and I just wanted for God to leave me alone. The atmosphere in the place was filled with God's presence. I knew He was pursuing me, just waiting for me to answer. The sawdust on the floor and wooden pews seemed to all fade away in those moments for me, I could feel God calling me, pulling at my heart, making it personal.

I sat there with my face in my hands, telling God, "No, it's going to require more than this for me to say yes." I prayed again, "I've been in these kinds of services my entire life God, you're not getting me this time." Just then the speaker pointed almost directly at me and said, "There's a young man here who doesn't want to go into ministry because he believes his dad was a failure at it. God's not telling you to be the same, He's simply asking you to say yes!" I couldn't' hold it in any longer, it felt like a ton of bricks was lifting off my chest. I was in a room with strangers, how could this guy know anything? I knew the Holy Spirit was calling out to me. The only sound I could hear was my heaving and crying. I must've laid down at that wooden altar for an hour before I finally said, "Yes God! Whatever you ask!" I surrendered my bitterness and resentment. It was like the floodgates opened and my desires in an instant were turned upside down.

God has this kind of experience for every believer. I know people react differently but the conviction is the same. The altar is not a place, it is an experience. At an altar you sacrifice your all, you give up and surrender your burdens, your filth, your ideas, your plans, your agenda, and ask God to give you His desires and His love. I had been so blind, but because of the altar I could see.

FOR WHAT IT'S WORTH

God gives every believer a mission in this world, do it.

- Plant your knees at the altar and your nose in the Word until you say 'yes' to God's call.
- God's call begins by being exclusive, Jesus is the only way to heaven.
- The mission will lead you on a narrow path, walk it faithfully.
- Your calling is expensive, expend it wisely.

"And immediately something like scales fell from his eyes, and he regained his sight."
Acts 9:18

High School Pain and Girl Power 4

My experiences with God and being in church was a sharp contrast to those I was having in high school. I think this still holds true for most church going students today; I don't think things have really changed that much. There are still cliques, bullies, and drugs everywhere, but compared to the culture of my home life and church, it was a lot to take in. I was getting a baptism of juiced-up teenage hedonism in the social experiment of high school. I suppose it is like any other part of the social experiment as massive amounts of people are thrown together into various environments such as work, school and government.

While God dominated my belief, there was still one thing specifically that distracted me - girls. I had been "going out" with a girl my junior year, thought she was the world, then we broke up. I never considered all the consequences and how this would impact the rest of that year. You see, we had signed up to share a locker together. Now we would be forced to share that locker even though we weren't "together." And seeing each other several times a day introduced increased tensions I wished I could avoid. Little did I know I would later marry that girl.

After we broke up, I started hanging out with my new flame and I went to see her every opportunity I could. I would make excuses to borrow a vehicle from Mom and Dad just so I could drive to Black Diamond, a few miles away, just to be with her. She was also a Christian and I really liked that about her. She invited me to go with her to hear this band that was playing and this preacher guy, none other than Josh McDowell. I knew who he was, our Youth Pastor played his videos in our youth group. However, neither of us could have expected or been prepared for what happened next. We found a seat in the second or third row and were holding hands when Josh McDowell came from behind and greeted us. The first thing he asked is, "Are you a couple?" For those of you who don't know Josh McDowell's ministry, at that time it was heavily into the message of abstinence, purity, and attaining certain goals before marriage. So here I am, seventeen years old, with my girl, and one of the foremost communicators on relationships in the world has just asked me, "Are you a couple?" My "girlfriend" quickly let go of my hand. "Um, we're dating", I said. He continued to make general conversation, asking us who we were and where we came from in order to be there that night. He thanked us for coming and moved on. That encounter made me genuinely consider what "dating" really meant. I didn't have to wonder about it very long, by the end of his presentation I was pretty certain that what I had in mind was not really what God had in mind or wanted.

The encounter with Josh McDowell really affected me in a big way. I was now wrestling with bigger concepts than just having a girlfriend. I had big questions to answer, like "is this a girl I want to marry?" And was sexual purity before marriage really one of my values? God used this encounter to force me to surrender these ideas in prayer. I believe my girlfriend had the same convictions and it didn't take us too long to figure out that there were other things we needed more than a boyfriend or girlfriend. It was God's guiding hand, helping me to focus on my relationship with Him. He rekindled the spark that Pam and I had for one another and in just a few short years we would be married.

God really protected me through all my teenage years. Pam and I both chose to honor God and respect His values where relationships were concerned, deciding to save ourselves for our wedding night, which has now been more than thirty years ago. We are not perfect people but God is gracious in understanding our weaknesses and gives us His strength in our greatest areas of temptation. This is one of the great messages that God uses the church to communicate to the world, He has another way! You don't have to follow the way of the world, media, and peers. Marriage between a man and a woman is God's foundation for the family. This message is antithetical to the popular worldview. Preachers should not be shy about teaching and preaching about sex and its benefits, blessings and misuses in this culture. Studies show that married Christian couples have better and more frequent sexual experiences than those who are not married. The significance of Biblical covenant marriage and sex should be taught with compassionate boldness to a generation that has been sold a bill of lies by pop culture. We have the message of salvation and it covers sex. The church should boldly and unashamedly uphold this standard.

FOR WHAT IT'S WORTH

Sexual temptation is real, add the qualities of virtue to your life

- Virtue is a threat to Satan, don't be surprised that he will provide attractive temptations.
- There is such freedom and enjoyment when a couple chooses to wait until marriage for sex. Married couples have better sex and more often than those who are unmarried.
- Don't be concerned if you are made fun of because of your virtue. Your critics are only ashamed in the presence of your power.

"... the body is not meant for sexual immorality, but for the Lord, and the Lord for the body." 1 Corinthians 6:13

Falling Out of Trees & Falling in Love

Doing fairly dangerous things as a kid transitioned into my teen years as well. One of those dangerous stunts nearly got me killed. I was at Pam's house when Alvin, her dad, asked me to help cut down a large tree on the edge of their driveway. The fir tree was about sixty feet tall and had lots of branches for climbing. So…

Tree climbing high above the ground;

No safety lines;

Very dangerous;

Potential for grievous injury;

I'm in!

I tied a short rope to a band saw and started climbing. The idea was to cut off about ten feet at a time from the top down. I sawed through the first two sections with ease. Pushing each section away from me, they fell over to the ground. When I got to the third section, about forty feet up, my saw bound up under the weight of the tree. Alvin threw a long rope up to me. I climbed a few feet above where I was cutting to tie the rope to the tree, high enough for Alvin to pull that section away from me. I was able to get the rope tied when Alvin said,

"Ready?"

"No!"

Alvin thought I said, "Go!" He began to pull the rope with me still above the cut! I could hear the crack of the tree trunk and soon found myself coming down with the tree as he pulled that section. Fortunately, I let go and was able to catch myself on some of the branches that were below me. Although I knew it was a misunderstanding, I would often tease Alvin that he did it because I was hanging around his little girl.

My desire to be around Pam only increased with time. If I knew she was going to be somewhere I would do my best to be there as well. Anything to be around her. The largest part of the time we spent together was in our youth group. It was a small group then, no more than a dozen or so, but they had a genuine desire to worship, pray, and seek God. Our youth pastor would plan all-night prayer meetings. We had a few of those back then. Although none of us could stay awake much later than 3:00 am, it was still impactful. We would have people come in each hour and lead a talk or a devotional. In between we would simply pray at the front of the church. I attribute my fervor for prayer today to my experiences at those altars and, of course, the youth camps. They changed me forever.

However, I must admit that prayer wasn't my only motivation for going to an all-night prayer meeting with a bunch of teenagers. Pam was there. It was at one of those prayer services that we started to have genuine feelings for each other. I couldn't imagine a better place to fall in love than at a prayer meeting. I couldn't get her out of my mind. She was in my every thought. I started writing love letters. I would go over to her house every opportunity I could. I was hooked, mesmerized, and captivated. I was certain from that point on, that one day, she would be my wife. And I'm sure that falling in love was better than falling out of a tree.

FOR WHAT IT'S WORTH

Prayer is vital for everything:

- You can be a minister without prayer but you cannot minister without prayer.
- Fervent prayer is a spiritual interaction, don't expect everyone to understand it. Only the genuinely saved person will identify because it is spiritually discerned.
- Get busy praying with and for your spouse, or your future one. God answers prayer.
- God is speaking a lot and doing it loudly, prayer opens our ears to hear what He is saying. There's never ever anything wrong with the broadcaster, only the receiver.

"There are three things that amaze me—no, four things that I don't understand: how an eagle glides through the sky, how a snake slithers on a rock, how a ship navigates the ocean, how a man loves a woman." Proverbs 30:18-19

"God's work done in God's way will never lack God's supplies"

Hudson Taylor

Swing Sets and Hammers

As I've already confessed, I really hated high school; I couldn't wait to get out, to say goodbye and good riddance. When I did, the first thing I did was pick up my tools and get a job. I learned really quickly that the world out there was nothing like high school. There are no excuses like, "the dog ate my homework" or "I overslept." I really enjoyed the challenge of being my own person, responsible for all my decisions, and was excited to be free from the clique-infested high school. It didn't take me long to find something I really loved. I had learned all kinds of stuff from Dad that kept me going; not just carpenter skills, but the intangible qualities like: punctuality, a good work ethic, and diligence. One thing I knew for sure, getting paid by the foot worked best for me. To get paid by the hour would have both financially and personally. I was enjoying making money and going to college at night, and it didn't take long for ministry to be in the rear-view-mirror. My job had given me the opportunity to move into my own house and set it up to my likin' and to get my own car and pay for a few extras along the way. Although I admit, I often went home for Mom's chili as-well-as almost anything else edible.

Another amazing thing gaining momentum in my life was my relationship with my future wife, Pam. We had been dating for a while and it was getting serious. One evening after work we went out to get some Mexican food. Afterward we went to an elementary school playground and sat on the swings. As we sat there on the swings we started talking about marriage and family. We had had conversations about it many times before, but this was more in the realm of "What would it be like?" or "If we ever got married…" I admit, I didn't plan this out very well. I didn't have the ring, the flowers, the band, or the perfect sunset, but I knew the time was right. "Pam, will you marry me?" Fortunately, she said yes. That was the easy part, the hard part came when talking to her dad.

Have you ever seen a cat play with a mouse? Tossing it around like some toy before it finally devours the creature? That's how I felt talking to Alvin, Pam's dad, when asking him for permission to marry his daughter. To make matters worse I had an audience. Pam was there along with her mother. I think having it televised to the entire world would have been easier. To this day I don't know why it was so difficult, after all we had been dating for a long time. "Alvin, I need to ask you something", I said. He replied, knowing what I was going to ask, "Yes, Larry, you have a question for me? I wonder what it could be. Come on now, I want to hear." Actually, I'm unsure of his exact words, I just know he was playing with this mouse. We went back and forth for a while until Pam just spoke up, "We're getting married!"

Alvin didn't seem shaken by the statement, he knew it was coming, but he sure enjoyed the show.

I had been an usher in weddings, asked to sing at several, and set up as many chairs for receptions as anyone, but I had never experienced having to help make the decisions for one. I remember my head almost splitting open from all the details at one point and wanted to just elope. I think Pam and I learned more about one another during that time than many other significant moments in our married life. We got our tiny little house ready, planned our honeymoon trip, and finished all the details of the ceremony.

The day finally arrived and all went according to plan for the most part; like most weddings including ours there was one little "oops". Our precious pastor forgot to say "You may kiss the bride". After a short pause Pam spoke up and said, "I want my kiss!" The pastor may have forgotten but she sure didn't. I didn't realize how draining the day would be and by the end of the reception we were exhausted.

I think most couples are, but at the end we took off, and never looked back.

We were young, nineteen when we got married, and it wasn't until seven years later that the kids started coming, and once they started, they kept coming and four boys later we were complete. If I had to record all the victories and struggles we faced, it would take more server space than Hillary's lost emails. But God has blessed us abundantly. We started as partners and have stayed partners through it all.

FOR WHAT IT'S WORTH

Having a partner for life is among God's greatest gifts to all of mankind.

- Companionship requires being there and being involved, so be there.
- Completeness through marriage contributes to overall contentment in life, enjoy it.
- Marriage is so important that God uses it as an illustration of Himself and the Church, treasure it.

"He who finds a wife finds a good thing and obtains favor from the Lord."
Proverbs 18:22

Misery or Missouri?

It didn't take us long to figure out that I needed to get some theological education if I was really going to pursue ministry. Pam and I loaded up, headed out, and landed in Springfield, Missouri just three days before our one-year anniversary in April, 1989. Our good friends, Ken and Melanie had finished school at Central Bible College in Springfield and were going to be heading into ministry soon. They let us stay with them for a few weeks until we were able to rent our own house. I started working at CBC right away on a dormitory renovation and Pam got a job at the Assemblies of God National Office.

Even though the first ten years of my life were in Michigan and Ohio, I had forgotten or repressed the memory of bugs. We just don't have them in Washington or Montana like they did here. We have spiders, sure, but that's just about it. But in Missouri, there's bugs everywhere; in the grass, in the air, in the trees, and on the windshields. The first house we rented was older and made our skin crawl on the very first night. We kept hearing scratching noises in the walls at night. I will never forget walking into the kitchen to get something from the frig and when I turned on the light, at least a thousand bugs just scattered! I had never really experienced cockroaches before that night, we had to do something. We told the landlady and she assured us that she would get the place bombed for bugs. The bugs won once again when we went horseback riding; when I got home, I had several ticks on my chest, belly and back not counting the ones elsewhere. Bugs, ugh! We eventually moved out of that house and were glad to wave the roaches goodbye.

Another anomaly that affected me more than Pam was the humidity and heat. If it gets above eighty degrees in the Puget Sound area, we swelter and complain how hot it is. But in the summer, Missouri gets hotter than a liberal at a women's rights march. We scraped our money together and went to this amazing place called Wal Mart, (It was kind of like a Kmart, but a little, um… nicer?) and we bought a fan.

We were so miserable that one night we actually soaked the top sheet of our bed in water and let the fan blow on us. We were frustrated, we were tired and we were alone. Finally, when almost asleep the fan started whining, at least I thought it was the fan. I got up, so upset, I started hitting the fan to make it stop when I realized it wasn't the fan making the noise. It was a siren across the street going off.

Fortunately, we had gotten the phone hooked up before we moved in, so I called Ken, "Hey, what's that siren for?" I asked. He said, "That's the tornado warning, you need to go to a safe place in the house." My experience with tornados was limited to what I had seen in movies or on television, and news reports where I had seen the aftermath of what they can do. We quickly huddled under our dining room table, wondering if we were about to be sucked out the chimney or something. I finally got our little T.V. hooked up and with enough foil on the rabbit ears, we were able to watch the news.

It wasn't till the next day that we learned the locals slept through the whole thing. I'm like, "This happens all the time?" It's like them asking if we were all safe from the volcano, I'm like, "What volcano?" They were talking about Mt. St. Helens. The news is usually scarier sounding and looking the further you get from the disaster. Between the bugs, tornados, heat and humidity, we really did think we were in misery but it was just Missouri.

The best thing about Missouri was the people; they were tremendous. Pam and I had such good friends at work and from the school, it was truly amazing. A friend of mine rented an apartment in the Zimmerman home and we spent a lot of time together. We even got to have a couple of dinners with Thomas and Elizabeth Zimmerman at their home in Springfield. He was the longest serving Superintendent of the Assemblies of God. His library was impressive with pictures of him with U.S. presidents and even a couple of movie stars. I really enjoyed being around the Zimmermans, they were so encouraging to us and really made us feel up to the task.

FOR WHAT IT'S WORTH

When you respond to God's call, welcome trouble.

- Don't react badly when facing hardship. The sirens of life are only meant to inform you of a problem.
- Listen to those who have walked this road before you, you stand on their shoulders.
- Obedience to God's call will always produce an inexhaustible strength.

"He gives power to the faint, and to him who has no might he increases strength"
Isaiah 40:29

Busted Pipes and Flooded Bookstores

"Base to one-ninety, we have an emergency", my radio sprang to life just an hour after I had gotten home. Pam and I lived just a few blocks from Central Bible College in Springfield, Missouri. I had been put in charge of a dormitory renovation at the ripe old age of twenty-one. I answered the radio and rushed back to the job having some idea of what had happened. When I arrived, my suspicions were confirmed. One of my crew asked me if he could work late and was installing a slop sink in the janitor's closet on a dorm room wing just above the campus bookstore. I have no idea why he did what he did, but he did it. The water supply lines were just a little too short so he attempted to force the valve up to help the hoses reach. Well, that can only go bad. Not only did it break, but the shutoff valve was located downstairs in the campus bookstore, which was closed and no one seemed to have the key.

After I spoke with my guy on-site, we ran downstairs and looked through the door window into the bookstore and it looked like a monsoon raining down on all the books and supplies. Ceiling tiles and insulation that had gotten saturated and fallen were scattered all over the floor. I called the security office and we were finally able to get in and turn off the valve, however it would be quite some time before the water would stop coming down. The water had already been running nearly an hour at this point.

I grabbed my guy and we ran back upstairs to check out the damage up there. I looked down the hallway and then in the room adjacent to the janitor's closet and oddly enough there was no sign of water. However, when I opened the closet door where the sink was located, the room had filled up with about two feet of water and I had just released the floodgates. The room was so tight and the carpet had swelled up so much it created a seal at the bottom, keeping the water in the small room.

Taking care of the damages wasn't the hard part, the hard part was calling Mr. Compton, the school's business manager and telling him what had happened. He said he would be right over. I thought for sure that I was going to be fired. We were working diligently to clean up the water and start some temporary repairs when he walked in. He looked around, walked up to me and simply said, "Larry, get this cleaned up."

I enjoyed our time at CBC. I learned how to run a large job with several employees. I also took advantage of the chapel services and some of the campus life. However, I learned more about ministry from serving in church than I ever did from Bible college. Peace Chapel was a church outside of Springfield that we attended and served in. Pam and I were involved in teaching a class, playing in the worship band and doing special music. The church was good sized, about a thousand people, but didn't feel that big. Pastor Blansit gave us a place to serve that fit us. We didn't mind leaving Missouri at all - so long bugs, tornados and humidity. But we hated leaving the church. Being a part of the worship team, teaching classes and a genuine sense of belonging were invaluable experiences for us.

FOR WHAT IT'S WORTH

You will mess up, keep moving forward.

- If you allow your present or past failures to consume you, it will alter your future.
- Never allow failure to make you stop. You will only lose the race if you quit running.
- Expect to do things that are hard. God will give you strength for your tasks, not just tasks fit for your strength.
- Endure discipline from your authorities with humility. No one likes to listen to someone with excuses.

"I press on toward the goal for the prize of the upward call of God in Christ Jesus."
Philippians 3:14

From Misery to Ministry

"AAAAHHHHH", Amy's screams echoed throughout the house. As her brother, I knew that scream, it was legit. I ran to the bathroom and there was Amy pointing to the invading creature, a spider. I quickly disposed of the intruder and Amy was saved. Pam and I were so grateful that Amy decided to come to Springfield and live with us. She worked at a nursing home near CBC and really helped us out. Money was tight and we were on our own, far from family and far from home. You know how it is, no matter where you go, home is always home and home is always better, even if it really isn't. I've gone swimming in the Caribbean, bounced around South America and Mexico, been to nearly every state, all of that's nice, but it's still not home.

I attended a chapel service at CBC one day and was really challenged to get going in ministry. Once again, I had gotten distracted from the call and started planning other things. Pam's uncle, Les Greaser, was a pastor in Winston, Oregon. I would talk to him from time to time. Since we moved to Washington, I had become acquainted with most of Pam's family and even spent time with Les in Oregon. One of our phone conversations began to venture into the realm of ministry and it wasn't too long and we were on our way, where I would work with him as his youth pastor in Oregon.

Another road trip with Amy! We had a trailer built, packed everything in it and headed west. I couldn't wait to get back to the West Coast and leave this place. Les sent us some money and we saved up what we could for the journey, which cost much more than we anticipated. In fact, when we got there, we quickly sold the trailer to get enough money to get into an apartment. We were so young, we were broke, and I was so senseless. And yet, we would receive much more than we could ever give. I knew there would be hard work, and I was prepared for that. However, the experiences of pastoral ministry magnified the significance of hospital visits, time spent listening to people talk about their struggles, and a heightened devotion to prayer. All of which helped to shape my character.

It didn't take me long to realize that being in real vocational ministry isn't all about building stuff, singing songs and preaching. During those years, from Les' example, I was confronted with my own lack of integrity in areas I really had never considered because they had never been confronted. My spiritual zeal, ministry of the Word or other typical "up front" functions were never the real problems, rather I faced very concerning challenges with honesty, relationships and authority. I was saved but my character sure wasn't. These issues made me genuinely contemplate if this was for me. Being a pastor is much more than preaching good sermons or spending enough time in prayer, (although there is no substitute), but if you really want to be a pastor you have to relate to people and bigger yet, you have to be completely transparent. People can see stuff you try to hide when you are in leadership. It will eventually come out. I learned more about myself and what would be required if I was going to move any further with this gig.

FOR WHAT IT'S WORTH

Jesus may have saved you but the Holy Spirit wants to work on your character.

- Character will advance your ministry and career much more than your education.
- People in authority give responsibility to the responsible.
- Do small things with excellence and integrity. God will give you bigger things after you have proven faithful with the small stuff.
- Always do what you ought to do, especially when you don't want to do it.

"The saying is trustworthy: If anyone aspires to the office of overseer, he desires a noble task. Therefore, an overseer must be above reproach..."
1 Timothy 3:1

From Drano Bombs to Maturity

Winston, Oregon is a small town on the outskirts of Roseburg. I remember the main industry in the area was logging. Roseburg Lumber is one the largest producers of plywood in the entire country. It is also home to "Wildlife Safari," a drive-through preserve that has everything from lions, grizzly bears, giraffes, to monkeys. It is a cool place. Winston was also my second youth pastor ministry experience. Along with my youth ministry responsibilities I led worship from time to time and was in charge of our Easter production. Which usually went well, except for one time.

"What happened?"

"Jesus didn't rise from the grave?"

I was bombarded with questions after a lighting problem at the Friday night performance of our Easter passion play. The whole church knew Jesus is supposed to rise from the grave, however, one of the girls from the youth group had forgotten to turn on the spot lights at the last stanza of "Rise Again." The lights were the cue for the stone to be rolled away and Jesus would come victoriously out of the cardboard tomb that we had built. Fortunately, He did rise from the grave on Saturday and Sunday night.

"Run before it blows!" I hollered to DeShane, the pastor's son. We had made a Drano bomb and threw it in the river upstream at a church picnic. (The right proportions of some crystal Drano, tin foil, and water in a two-liter soda bottle creates so much joy.) It blew big! Water shot up into the air and terrified people ran from the beach. We sauntered in to the picnic a couple hundred feet away as if nothing had happened. I thought it was awesome! Not everyone agreed. Many people thought it was childish. It was.

Being a youth pastor can be a lot of fun and keep you young. DeShane was more buddy than student to me during those years, and kept me young in heart and actions. I was more kid than youth pastor, especially in the beginning. Poor Les. I believe my senior pastor had his hands fuller with me than anyone. Besides the growing pains of being a youth pastor and learning responsibility, Winston gave Pam and me opportunities to do things we had never done before.

"Don't do drugs!" We all shouted at the end of a skit we had performed for the Winston Jr. High School student body and faculty. I had been able to assimilate a group of local youth leaders in the community and start an on-campus outreach. Getting involved with the youth in the community meant going where they were, which also meant that I tutored in band at both the junior and the senior high schools, and I led some school rallies with short dramas and talks. I helped in a special education class at the high school, coached seventh-grade basketball at the Christian school, and was fairly connected with my fellow youth pastors in the area. Being this involved taught me numerous things about ministry, people, and myself. Being involved gave me the chance to mature and grow while working in ministry and making a difference. All these were great experiences as a result of being in Winston.

My Senior Pastor, Les, was so patient with me in those days and I was able to do a lot of things that centered on my talents. We renovated parts of the building, did some framing on the parsonage garage, pulled weeds, pulled weeds, and we pulled weeds. I don't think that weed pulling is one of my gifts, but I think Les thought so. We also led worship services, went on our first foreign mission's trip. Les had me preach occasionally and I played my horn. Les pretty much forced me to finish my educational requirements, only because I went kicking and screaming. However, I am so glad he did, and I value that; but I appreciate the coaching for ministry and the experiences of my time in Winston even more. I learned how to deal with difficult people, love the unlovely, and, most importantly, how to truly serve with no expectations of appreciation or trophies like I had been accustomed to.

I think it would have been easy for us to stay in Winston after Les and Joyce got some of my kinks worked out, at least the big ones.

The problem was that he let me preach. It was all downhill from there. I was driven to preach all the time and it only got more compelling. I had, and still have, an almost insatiable drive to speak God's word, without a filter. The passion has only grown over time. Having been in vocational ministry for more than twenty-eight years at this point, it is tough to imagine ever stopping. There may be a day, we will see.

Les and Joyce are among some of the true heroes of the church. They weren't looking for notoriety or wealth, that's for sure. Simply to serve. Small church pastors are extremely resilient and driven. Discouragements do come, people are broken. They can betray you, and sometimes be vindictive. Most of the time however, they know they are loved by these incredible people who accept the challenge of pastoring a small church.

FOR WHAT IT'S WORTH

Being humble is required for life and an absolute necessity in ministry.

- People will be difficult, get used to it. The problem is always pride; it is the source of all contention.
- If you refuse to humble yourself, God will put people in your life eager to help you become humble.
- Never expect to get recognized for serving, God is the One who will reward you.
- All of the great people in Scripture were great because they counted on God being with them.

"If you pick up a starving dog and make him prosperous, he will not bite you. This is the principle difference between a dog and a man."
Mark Twain

"He is no fool who gives what he cannot keep, to gain what he cannot lose."

Jim Elliot

Chasing Sheep and Baby Boys

"You stupid, #@%& sheep!" I think I can in fact count on both hands how many times I've uttered those words in my life. Not because I am good, it's not something I was raised around and it's not in my necessary vocabulary. I had been chasing these stupid sheep around for an hour so the buyer could load them in his truck and take them away. The owners of the property we were renting from lived on the East Coast and asked us to make the deal for them. The house was outside of Enumclaw on a large piece of land with a pond, lots of trees and a picture-perfect view of Mt. Rainier. I had gotten a carpenter job in the Seattle area before we left Winston. Pam loved feeding the sheep and the horse that we took care of. I was not loving getting them into the truck; it was a dirty, disgusting chore and made more maddening by the stupidity of the sheep. I finally managed to get all the sheep into the pickup truck which had tall plywood sides, with the agonizing exception of one. Yes. Of course, one. All the sheep needed shearing badly and had matted mud and feces on their undercarriage. Did I say disgusting?

I was reminded of Jesus leaving the ninety-nine and going after the one. I never knew sheep were much more difficult to catch! (There's a sermon in there somewhere.) I chased that sheep around the pond, back to the main house, down the driveway, and back into the pasture. I was finally able to corner it between the barn and back of the truck. Sweaty and frustrated, I dove in for the kill. As I picked him up by the wool, he bit me on the ankle! I was beyond frustrated. I was furious! I lifted him up. Like Hulk Hogan body slamming Andre the Giant, I threw him in the back of the truck. I know it was quite a scene when the new owner looked at me.

"Feel better?"

Maybe he was concerned that I had damaged the merchandise. I didn't care. My job was done, and I was glad I didn't have to deal with any more sheep. At least not the four-legged kind.

Once farm life settled down, Pam and I thought it was time to start a family. We had been married six years at that point, life was good. Secular employment offered more money, insurance, and security than ministry could, that was for sure. I could go to my job, work alone, and get paid by production. I loved it! I've only had three full time jobs in my life where I was paid by the hour; one after high school, one during our CBC days and a carpenter job I had while being a senior pastor. I enjoyed getting paid by the foot, the harder you worked the more money you made. It fit me somehow, I like the production world much more than the hourly or salaried one.

"Let's go for a walk." Pam would often say when I got home. Being more than eight months pregnant with our first baby was so exciting. We went to the hospital a couple of times with false alarms, thinking "This was it!" Finally, it wasn't a false alarm; "This was IT!" We rushed to the hospital and got into the room. Pam's contractions were getting closer and closer. We were praying, I was rubbing her back, I was excited and a little scared at the same time. Then we heard the woman in the next room screaming at her counterpart, "You did this to me you &@#%!". Pam and I looked at each other and chuckled a little, well, for half a second or so. Pam was great. No bleeped bleeps came from her.

I have had the privilege of being there, and even helping, at the delivery of all my boys. There is nothing like it. When they handed Brandon to me, he was crying, until I spoke. He seemed to strain toward my voice. Pam and I cried; we were so happy. This event would repeat itself three more times and each time it would be a boy. There would be more testosterone in our home than there are snowflakes at a university campus protest rally. Each time we were elated. We continue to enjoy and be enriched by the amazing relationships we have with these godly and talented men.

FOR WHAT IT'S WORTH

Sheep bite, they smell bad, and will lay down and let a coyote eat them. You must protect them.

- If you are a pastor you are an under-shepherd to the Great Shepherd, take care of His flock.
- Do not get offended when they run away from you. Your faithfulness will ultimately help them hear God's voice.
- Your people are being attacked from every side, provide a refuge for them.

"All we like sheep have gone astray; we have turned every one to his own way; and the Lord has laid on him the iniquity of us all."
Isaiah 53:6

From Interim to Pastor

I thought I could handle working, building a business, and being a dad. Life felt good. We were renting a little duplex in Enumclaw, wanting to buy a house, attending and volunteering at church. However, I wasn't happy. I was being convicted by the Holy Spirit.

"What are you doing here? I have a mission for you." I had begun to believe that I had failed as a youth pastor. I began to ask myself. . . .

"What makes me think I would want to do this again?"

"Why would God think I could do this?"

I reached out to the Oregon Ministry Network. There were three churches that didn't have pastors at the time. I could go to one of them. The pastor at the church in Enumclaw was also encouraging. He gave me a list of churches in Washington State that were looking for a senior pastor.

At this point we were twenty-six years old and I honestly thought we were too young for any church to even look at us. Even so, we made a list of twelve churches, sent out eight resumes, and got eight calls for interviews. We prayed about it and we determined to follow through with three of them. I went alone to the first interview. Pam vetoed it when I got home. We went together to the second one. We truly thought this was the place, but we were keeping options open. The third place was Tacoma, our last pick of the litter. We had no interest in going to Tacoma. When we would go to Tacoma, we always left saying, "Boy, I would hate to live there." The church was in the Lakewood area of Tacoma. Now Lakewood is its own city. It was far smaller than the church we wanted to go to. It was not our first choice. However, God was changing our heart and He was giving us a real love for this place. We called the other church back and asked them to withdraw our names for consideration.

We went to the Lakewood interview and were grilled with questions, mostly doctrinal ones. There were nine of us in the room, the meeting was led by one of the board members who was in charge of the transition. Looking back, I've often wondered how difficult the process must have been for all of them. It was a little awkward, but the people were quite nice and we felt respected and wanted. I later learned that my resume was actually pulled back out of the trash.

The next day I got a phone call. We were asked to come and preach on a Sunday morning, "no strings attached," to get an idea of what we were like. Once we passed the preaching test we were invited to "try out". A try out is a big deal, if you make it this far that means you have squeezed through their filter and are worthy of further examination. Just like my dad's tryout so many years before.

They had a pot-luck that afternoon to have a chance for people to talk to us and check us out. That evening we preached again, then came time for the members to vote on us. They led us up to the pastor's office where we waited for them to vote. I have to admit I was apprehensive and a little nervous. Pam and I thought that everything went well and we had peace about the whole setting. After about thirty minutes the lead board member opened the door and said, "Welcome to Abundant Life, Pastor Larry!" That was more than twenty-four years ago.

Honestly, I would have never thought I would be in any place this long. I am surprised that I survived; because at first, I was terrible. I was still wearing my youth pastor/preacher hat and I was following an incredibly talented pastor who did a great job. My learning curve was about to become quite steep.

Small church leaders know their churches; this is one of the great advantages they have. Their ability to meet needs on a personal level is unparalleled. Because of this, pastors of small churches are the backbone of Christendom. This is an overlooked value among many denominational leaders. The pastors of these churches should have leadership support, assistance, and counsel for the duration of their ministry, not only when things go badly.

FOR WHAT IT'S WORTH

Selecting a pastor for their church is a big deal to your people, respect that.

- Do not compare what you have done before to what they are able to do now.
- Be faithful to God's word in teaching and preaching, you will earn their respect.
- Avoid situations where by-laws or policies require you to be voted on every year or so, you will lose the ability to get any traction for growth.

"Strengthening the souls of the disciples, encouraging them to continue in the faith... And when they had appointed elders for them in every church, with prayer and fasting they committed them to the Lord in whom they had believed."
Acts 14:22-23

Scuba and Diapers

My first challenge being a "Senior Pastor" of a church was - I HAD NO IDEA WHAT I WAS DOING! My biggest mistake was trying to figure out what the church had been doing rather than preparing for what it should be doing. I called the former pastors to get an idea of their experiences here. I gathered the Board for a meeting and was able to familiarize myself with where the church was financially. I also had a staff meeting to see what each person's job was in the church.

In spite of the fact that there were holes in vision-casting and connections, half the church apparently had left before I showed up. I knew how to preach and I knew how to sing. That was about the extent of it. I stuck with that as much as possible. However, preaching, no matter how good, will only get you so far. I struggled with some of the staff. Eventually, all but one found other places to serve. What was left was an amazing group of people who were supportive and we were encouraged by them.

One Sunday I was preaching about reaching out and used an illustration that would haunt me for a long time.

"God gives some people sickles and they reap a little, but to others God gives great, big, huge 'concubines.' No matter what, we have to use what we've been given." I meant to say "combines" and not "concubines."

It was quiet for a moment until from the back came,

"Did you say concubines?"

Needless to say, laughter erupted until I finally caught on. I'm unsure how we finished the service but from that point on the sermon was pretty much over.

One of our real struggles was money. The third month I was there I remember coming home with a paycheck that was less than half of what was promised. Pam assured me it would be fine. There was a budget back then of a certain amount for our salary, but for those first few years, we received the leftovers. After a few months, we had to sell my diving equipment to pay the rent and buy diapers. It didn't take long for me to start building houses again. I felt like quitting. I didn't want to be bi-vocational. I didn't know it then but for seventeen out of twenty-four years (so far,) I would work outside of the ministry full-time. At times it was my fault; I took salary cuts to hire extra staff members.

Back then the church was more than seventy-percent military which had an effect on the church. We love our military people. They always jump right in and contribute so much. The hard part is when they move away. That's when I learned that churches are built on influence, not position. The power of influence is definitely more significant than the power of position, ask any married man. One thing about the military, they never have to worry if the business brought in enough money, or if they were going to be able to afford health insurance, or pay their utility bill. However, to us, those years were like a yoyo. The church went up and down with the military deployments and PCS's (Permanent Change of Station). I loved the people, but I hated the life that I was forced to live at the time and wanted desperately to leave the ministry.

I would have given anything to have had some other pastors call and ask me how things were going or simply pray with me. God sent Dad. He would call me from time to time to tell me he was praying for me or show up out of the blue to have lunch. He was a life-saver. I knew he understood what I was experiencing and I valued his encouragement. I wish I had the chance to go back and tell him how much that meant. I also had a great board member that encouraged me constantly. When you are the pastor of a small church, you pour yourself into people and the work you are doing, but it takes a toll. Pastors can't bear this by themselves and need encouragement.

FOR WHAT IT'S WORTH

Make sure you meet the needs of your family first.

- Although the church may have great needs that you can meet, wait until it can produce for itself.
- If you begin to sacrifice too much of your family's security, your children may resent the ministry as they grow.
- When you model the priority of your family, your church will notice and grow to respect and support it.

"Therefore encourage one another and build one another up, just as you are doing."
1 Thessalonians 5:11

Preaching to Cats

"Can you make out this letter?" The secretary handed me a note one Sunday morning. It was barely legible. All we could decipher from the bad handwriting was a couple of words.

"I don't have any idea what this says, it looks like a kid wrote it or something." So, we threw it in the trash.

"Meow."

"Meow."

"Did you hear that?"

We heard a cat as we were working in the office the next day. I have no idea what the deal is with me and cats, nevertheless, we were hearing a cat. Outside the foyer, was a stray cat. Well, we thought it was a stray cat.

"What do you want me to do with it?" The church secretary asked me.

"I have no idea, maybe it will go away."

Well, it didn't. It hung around outside the front doors until Wednesday night.

It was a warm summer Wednesday evening; the front doors were open as I started to speak. We often had latecomers for the Wednesday night services. They would come in quietly and sit in the back. This latecomer did not sit quietly but came boldly strolling down the center aisle, like a bride drawing all attention to herself boldly crying out,

"Meow."

"Meow."

One of the people picked it up and took it back outside, but it came right back in with the same bold announcement.

Thursday I was at a jobsite framing a house. I jumped in my truck to eat lunch. Back in 1999, cell phones were huge, I think they gave you cancer if you held them to your head too long. The secretary called me and said the cat was back and asked me what I wanted to do.

"Call the pound."

I didn't figure there was anything more we could do, maybe someone would adopt it. At the very least it would be out of our hair.

After service that following Sunday, I was at the door greeting people as they were on their way out. A woman and her adult son approached me. They were difficult to understand, they spoke softly and mumbled. However, I caught the five words they repeated over and over again.

"Have you seen our cat?"

My heart sank.

I knew what they were talking about. Once we were able to have a conversation with them, we learned that they had left us a note saying they were going to visit relatives and wanted us to take care of their cat. Once I told them what happened, they just walked off. I felt so badly and was ready to take them to the shelter. I still wonder if they ever got their cat back. After we realized what the situation was, the secretary found the note in the garbage. We were able to decipher what it said.

"Please take care of our cat. We will be gone."

I guess I did.

FOR WHAT IT'S WORTH

Pastors of small churches are heroes because they often do things that no one else will do.

- Humbly accept responsibility for some small things early, later you will eventually have a cast of people willing to take those from you.
- Never forget that you really do produce who you are, so be like Jesus.
- Don't ask God if it is His will to do something when the plow is already in your hand.
- Live out your calling. God gave it to you; He will equip you to carry it out.

"I desire to do your will, O my God; your law is within my heart." Psalm 40:8

Rumor Weeds and Biting Sheep

"What are you going to do about it? I'm sick of all your @$%&!" Being a pastor of a small church, especially one that was largely military, is not without its fun. Our church had less than seventy people at the time. I had been called to a home on the airbase by a husband whose wife was pointing a gun at him. I don't know what possessed me to do it, but I stepped in between them and asked her to put the gun down. Imagine my relief when she agreed. Through a lot of discussion and prayer I was able to get them to come to an understanding. (Fun times.) Shortly afterward they got a new duty station and I never saw them again. One thing can be said, you never know what situation you will be called to help with; and in a small church as the senior, often only pastor, you get a chance to see it all.

"Why don't you guys come with us?" It seemed like each time we went on vacation we would take a third of the church with us camping somewhere. One couple went with us a few times and we developed a significant bond. She worked in the office with us and he was on our board. They became such good friends and we shared great times together. But soon enough the inevitable happened, they got a new duty station and moved away.

Although the stories and depth of relationships varied, this scenario was a broken record for us, "...they got a new duty station and moved away." We love our military people, but building a church with such a transient crowd is tough; to say nothing of losing friends to hang out with, pray with, and just do life together. Nearly fifty percent of our community moves every four years, we are saturated with military. More than sixty cents of each dollar spent in Lakewood is military money. They say leaving is always harder on the ones left behind, that was so true for us. Each time the turnover happened we had to rebuild the church. Sometimes this was so much easier said than done. Pam and I were worn out, burned out, and wanted out. As wonderful as military people are, this is not their home. Eventually, they leave and go back to wherever home is. Interestingly enough, at least from our experience, it is usually back to the Midwest. However, a changing church afforded me the longevity I've had because I've been able to make some pretty big mistakes and carry on. More often than not, when mistakes are made the pastor is the one who leaves. In our situation, because of the military turnover, the congregation of the church left more often. I was able to stay and work things through; surviving a transient church situation. I learned some important and valuable lessons along the way.

Just as we were about to give up hope, some local people from our community started to attend our church. It was an amazing time at first, we needed the help and we were so excited to have someone who wouldn't be moving at military's whim. (I didn't think a little transfer-growth could hurt.) Through our outreach, others came and we experienced a time of growth. During this period of new growth, the baptismal tank was busy, multiple services were happening, and involvement was great. However, I was soon reminded that sheep can bite.

Pam and I had four boys from 1995 to 2000, it was a busy time for us. At one point, three of the boys were in diapers at the same time. We changed diapers for eight straight years. I was working outside the church and keeping up with a growing church as best we could. We were always busy coming and going, our home was always full of friends and family. Exhausted but happy; to us all was going well. We were playing games one night with some church friends when they told us the first of many rumors. I couldn't believe it at first. There were nasty little things that people were saying about both Pam and me. Stupid things - things that most people would probably agree to disagree about, or at least accept the other person's view. At the time the church had a large group that preferred home schooling. The public-school parents started saying things about home schooling. As these things go, the other side said some things as well. It was all pretty foolish. However, instead of settling it as Christians should, rumors started growing and finally were dumped on us. It might have been a childish reason, but more than anything, it was hurtful. I couldn't believe how adults could say such things and sow discord that would be so damaging and bite so hard.

When the world looks at the church and sees such nonsense, they roll their eyes at our stupidity. A wise pastor told me once to always be proactive rather than reactive, I learned it too late. Not only did I not confront the situation properly, I tried to balance everyone's expectations and lost. Then I tried to deal with it covertly from the pulpit. I preached sermons toward specific people and the issues they were causing. THIS IS A TERRIBLE IDEA! NEVER DO THIS!

Small church pastors are heroes because they love people no matter what they do. If you pastor a larger church and someone disagrees or talks about you over lunch, no big deal, you don't have to deal with it. But small church pastors have had to grow thick skins and still be willing to wash the feet of their personal Judases.

"Our greatest fear should not be of failure but of succeeding at things in life that don't really matter."

FOR WHAT IT'S WORTH
Love the hurting, be patient with the vulnerable, confront the troublemakers.

- People will come and go. Never take it personally when they leave.
- The steadfast part of a church in a transient community might only be you. That's ok! Faithfulness has its own rewards.
- Privately, with grace confront trouble-makers. Backbiters and gossips sow discord, the Bible says God hates that.
- Work out your words before you confront. Wait until you have a plan. Discretion is knowing when best to say nothing at all.
- Remember that backbiters and gossips are called simple-minded in scripture.

"You shall not go around as a slanderer among your people, and you shall not stand up against the life of your neighbor: I am the Lord. You shall not hate your brother in your heart, but you shall reason frankly with your neighbor, lest you incur sin because of him. You shall not take vengeance or bear a grudge against the sons of your own people, but you shall love your neighbor as yourself: I am the Lord." Leviticus 19:16-18

Boards and Dads

I tried my best to focus my efforts on the church while building a business on the outside. This didn't work out so well. I felt divided and longed to devote all of my time to the church; so, early in 2001, I decided to quit working. I told the church board my plans. They decided to put the churches' best efforts into making my salary livable, without any outside income, while also maintaining current staffing. Working outside the church, I was able to make more than double the money, in addition to a retirement plan, health insurance, and various other benefits the church couldn't match. It was a tough decision but we put away the blue collar. We somehow made it work for four years; but with the growth of our family, and the desire to move forward financially, something had to give. I started working with my brother, just a little bit, on the side. That is where it started. This small step would soon get me into big trouble.

After a while of working both sides again I received a phone call,

"Pastor, can you come to the church? We want to have a meeting." One of my board members called me on a Thursday evening.

"What's up? Who wants to have a meeting?"

"The board is here and we want to discuss something with you." I was a little confused. Everything at church was moving forward during this time. I had a good relationship with them, so I went over to hear what this was about. They were concerned about me, working outside the church, and wanted me to stop. From my perspective, it was crazy! I told them that I would work from time to time and it would be fine. They should consider their jobs, wages and benefits compared to mine. Nonetheless, I agreed to slow it down.

On my way home from the meeting, I grew more and more out of sorts. I called Dad and gave him an earful. My attitude was pathetic. I was angry!

"How can they even compare my wages to the things that we do at the church?" I rambled on, "Did they forget the salary I am deferring to pay our youth pastor?" I kept going. Dad just listened. After some time, he simply said,

"Larry. God has grown the church there. Do you believe He has called you there?"

"Yes," was my begrudging answer. (Did I mention a pathetic attitude?) Then he said something that I treasure to this day.

"The needs of your family are first, but that means that God will meet your needs where you are."

I didn't like that answer.

I shared with one of the board members what was going on with me and that I was looking at other churches. He asked me not to leave. Pam and I applied at another church in our state. They had a congregation of seven-hundred and wanted to build a new building. I couldn't be more thrilled. I thought this was the time. I went to the interview and was once again bombarded with questions. They had listened to some sermon tapes I had supplied them and wanted me to come and preach on Sunday. I agreed. Needless to say, I didn't take the position. It was not what God wanted for us. Pam had an uneasy feeling about the place we interviewed, that it wasn't right for us. We learned a short time later that the church had gone through a huge split and there was major fallout. We were spared. Through all this God had us where he wanted us, even if we were not happy with it at the time.

FOR WHAT IT'S WORTH

Church leaders are important and should be chosen based on their influence.

- The power of influence is always greater than the power of position. Just ask any woman's husband.
- Never keep your leaders in the dark about big stuff in your life and church business. Leaders will serve with you well if they have adequate information.
- You must build relationships with your leaders that goes beyond average. They will trust who they know.

"The saying is trustworthy: If anyone aspires to the office of overseer, he desires a noble task." (1 Tim 3:1)

Dads and Devic's

Answering the phone, I never expected to hear Amy frantically say, "Larry, Dad went in the ambulance to the hospital!" Pam and I scrambled to get the kids ready and ran out the door. We rushed to Enumclaw and picked up Amy and Mom. We finally got to the hospital and into the waiting room, we asked the nurse where he was. Everything was such a blur. They took us to a different room at first, then finally led us to where Dad was. Dan, my brother, was standing beside the bed, but Dad was already gone. I remember it so vividly.

"No!" Amy cried out.

As for myself, I didn't know what to feel. I think I was numb with shock. Dad had a rare disease called Devic's Syndrome, or NMO, which acts similar to A.L.S. (Lou Gehrig's Disease), rapidly eating away at nerve cells in the brain and spinal column bit by bit. Here laid my strong, dependable, and gracious father, taken out one year after diagnosis by a disease we had never heard of.

The new sanctuary in Enumclaw, which Dad had built, was packed for the funeral. Dad's siblings had flown in from Michigan, Missouri, and California to be there. My brother and I built his casket out of solid oak, the wood he often used in his shop. His brothers sprayed the lacquer, his sisters made the inside linens, pillows, and inner lid décor. I didn't cry in the hospital. I hadn't had any reaction during the funeral planning, or any other time so far. It wasn't until we started cutting the wood for the casket and I smelled the sawdust, that I was overwhelmed with emotion. I was taken back to the places I had been with him, doing carpentry work on a building somewhere in the past. I remembered thinking how unfair it would be for my boys to not have a grandpa and for me not to have anyone to lean on anymore.

I often called my dad through all of those years when I was a senior pastor. I had been such a crazy teenager, but as a young dad and a pastor he was so comforting in spite of my ups and downs. He shaped and guided my ability to be faithful to God's call no matter what. I have read a lot of books, and have had solid theological training. I appreciate my education; I have gleaned great things from them. However, my father was my greatest influence and hero, even when I acted like he wasn't. I wouldn't trade that for all the books in the world. I know he wasn't perfect, super-educated, or "successful," (as many church leaders would define success today), but he was more faithful and determined and a far better preacher than most. What I admired about him more than anything wasn't the six-foot-four-inch, suit-wearing, smiling professional-looking pastor, but rather I admired his blue-collar. He was a fighter. He endured the financial hardships of small church ministry, he remained faithful when things were most difficult, he lovingly and strongly confronted naysayers and he always cast a vision in spite of tough circumstances. He was unafraid to go against the flow. In a day where seminaries may produce ministers looking for the high-paying, large-ministry positions, we need more blue-collar pastors like him.

FOR WHAT IT'S WORTH
The leaders of yesterday's church and our elders deserve our respect and admiration, no matter the size of their churches or their popularity.

- Celebrate the pastors that may be attending your church, retired or otherwise. They have endured the situations and scenarios, and many more issues than I have written in this book.
- The heritage of their families leaves a mark. Pastors produce pastors.
- The passing of one of our patriarchs is not only reason to celebrate, but to grieve, for the world has lost an ambassador of Christ.
- Take time to listen to their stories, they'll get around to the point eventually. Show respect by listening to what they have to say.

"Do not rebuke an older man but encourage him as you would a father."
1 Timothy 5:1

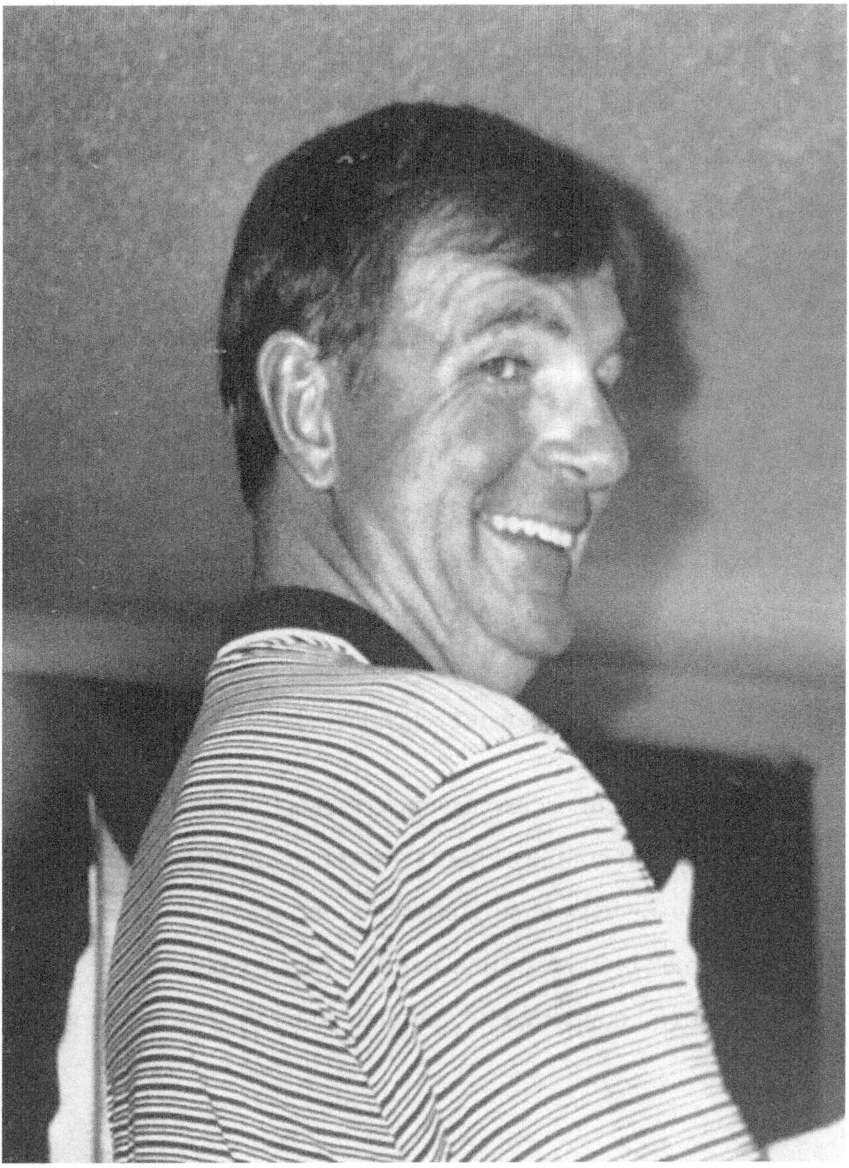

Heart Attacks and Priorities

It was my birthday, September 19th, 2012, but something wasn't quite right. I was managing construction projects outside the church; I was responsible for controlling twenty jobs or more, at once. I was coordinating my crews, scheduling substitutions, and working with homeowners. It was exhausting. All the while I was a "full-time" pastor with a staff and a busy church schedule. Something needed to change and it was about to give in a big way.

The Saturday before my birthday I had gotten food poisoning at a wedding reception. I was terribly sick for three days. I got up the next morning, and started getting ready for work; I sat down on the bed. I was weak and had a burning sensation in my chest. Initially, I thought it was heartburn, but quickly realized this was bigger than last night's burritos. I started to slump over when Pam caught me and called in the boys. They carried me to the car and drove straight to the emergency room. By this time, I was nearly incapacitated.

The pain in my chest became so severe I believed I was going to die. Over the next couple of hours, doctors administered as many pain-relieving drugs as was legally possible, but my chest was still on fire. They performed blood tests and five EKGs. I passed them all. No sign of heart attack. I continued to complain about the fire in my chest, but they could not give me any more medication. A heart surgeon was called in to evaluate me. He had me rushed into the operating room to do an ultra-sound on my heart. His words shocked me at first.

"Mr. Ellis, you have a ninety-five percent blockage in your LAD vein that comes out of your heart, we call it the "widow-maker". It is the vein that moves the most blood in your heart. If you choose to go home, you will probably die, unless I do surgery and soon." I had about as much choice as a liberal would have voting for Obama.

I was awake for the surgery. It was quite a novel sensation. I watched on the monitor as the surgeon pushed a stint all the way from my groin area, to my chest, and finally into my heart. I stayed in the hospital for three days. I was incredibly sick the entire time. I know that God was trying to get my attention. I was trying to provide for the needs of the church with my own strength, not through faith in Him to provide. That is not what God had in mind. The church had grown and the finances were more stable. I could have received more money from the church and quit working so much, even the doctor wanted me to take two weeks off. But I ignored his advice. I went to work the day after I got back home from the hospital.

During the following weeks, I moved slowly. I was blessed by my church, but I was flooded with the strange feeling of being alone.

My secular employment paid me double time for two weeks. I was surrounded by my family, and Pam never left my side.

I missed my Dad.

His pastor's heart would have brought so much encouragement and a good shoulder to cry on. I had a hard time figuring out what was happening to me. Was it post-traumatic-stress of some kind? My feelings were confusing me. I was emotional and short tempered after this event. I had resolved in the ER that I was ready to go to heaven. I had no doubt, but what I needed was a pastor.

I thought my denominational leaders would send someone, or maybe call, but they didn't. It was the faithful prayers and counsel of Pam and the love of my boys that gave me comfort and helped me make sense of it all. Being so close to death's door made me realize the priorities that I had been ignoring for way too long. I had traded time with God for preparing sermons. I had made time for a second job but neglected caring for my people. My dreams were just that, MY dreams. I was doing my will not His will. I had lost the most important thing any Christ-follower could lose - God-given vision.

At the writing of this book, I have not had a full-time secular job for four years. Since then the church has doubled its income and nearly doubled its attendance. I'm unsure if the church would still be considered "small." To me it doesn't matter. That's a categorization I leave to denominational leaders and church growth "experts." If you are a pastor of a small church, the big stages in this world may never call you a hero for what you do, or celebrate your ministry. I do know that America needs more pastors to flood this country with their thick skin, and their willingness to be dangerous enough to take a risk and be pioneers.

FOR WHAT IT'S WORTH

Take care of yourself, you are only getting older.

- Those close to you want you around as long as possible.
- Bi-vocational pastors must understand the priorities of their family.
- Be careful not to overdo it. Better to live in a shack and drive a beater than be gone too early.

"The Lord bless you and keep you; the Lord make his face to shine upon you and be gracious to you; the Lord lift up his countenance upon you and give you peace."
Numbers 6:24-26

MORE "For What It's Worth" from a Blue-Collar Pastor
(Wisdom for life and ministry)

Be Proactive Rather Than Reactive:

- Do everything you can to first get a clear vision with a plan of action. A "Plan B" implemented is better than doing nothing at all.
- Cast the vision and stick to the plan. If you don't cast the vision someone or some circumstance will cast one for you.
- Confront issues as soon as they start. A pot will only come to a boil if you leave it on the heat. Remove the heat before the person and the ministry are too hot to handle.
- Remember it is always easier to ask someone to join the band than to leave it. Make sure you know the capability of people before you put them into any leadership position. Better to utilize people in their gifts than to ruin their potential by putting them in places where they have no influence.
- Plan well for everything so there are easy steps for people to follow. Clarity is key.

- Ask yourself, in each situation, if this were to go sideways or people react poorly how could I avert it? People are messy, don't wait to react to a problem, do your best to preempt them.

Early on, we had people come from other churches to check out the new pastor. Many of them were wolves looking for a pastor and flock to devour. There are people looking to make trouble. I could have avoided many heartaches if I had been more proactive. It is equally important to connect with other ministers and build relationships with them. Don't wait for denominational or corporate leadership of your church to make this happen, they generally wait till the church is in trouble before they will do anything.

We are called to make disciples first. This is important because disciples are never disciples alone. That cannot be accomplished if we are not disciples ourselves. There are no Lone Ranger Christians, only lonely ones if they go at the ministry without the wisdom and coaching of those who have either walked or are walking that road as well.

"And, apart from other things, there is the daily pressure on me of my anxiety for all the churches." (2 Cor 11:28)

Know Your People:

- Small church ministry requires loving those that God has entrusted to you to love. Be willing to show your hand because they will certainly show you theirs.
- Minister to the people you have, not the ones you wish were there. Preach and teach with clarity to challenge those given to you, they will become the ambassadors to your community.
- You will not only be a better preacher by knowing your audience, you will be a better person by knowing your people.
- Be patient and content. If you are not content your people will not be content either. Too many pastors leave the ministry or leave too early. God is the One who builds the church.

Read:

- Read books about doctrine, church ministry, and other fun stuff. Throw out the bad, keep the good.
- If you don't read and continue to do so, it won't matter your degree or lack of them, you will not grow as a minister - of that I am convinced.
- Reading increases your ability to reach a wider audience and creates confidence in ministry.

Abundant Life Church is located in Lakewood, Washington, a semi-urban area south of Tacoma, close to Joint Base Lewis-McCord. There are a dozen churches around us that have more than a thousand people attending them, all within a thirty-minute drive. How does a church under two hundred people measure its effectiveness? By working to produce genuine followers of Jesus that share His love and grace in their community.

We first understand that God has given us our unique people and resources and put us where we are to simply do this mission. We are determined to love God, thrive in life, connect with others, to serve our world, and lead others in that process.

Made in the USA
Middletown, DE
10 May 2021